ALSO BY MILO FRANK

How to Get Your Point Across
in 30 Seconds—or Less

HOW TO RUN A SUCCESSFUL MEETING

—IN HALF THE TIME

Milo O. Frank

SIMON AND SCHUSTER

NEW YORK LONDON TORONTO SYDNEY TOKYO

Simon and Schuster
Simon & Schuster Building
Rockefeller Center
1230 Avenue of the Americas
New York, New York 10020

SIMON AND SCHUSTER and colophon are registered trade-marks of Simon & Schuster Inc.

Designed by Irving Perkins Associates
Manufactured in the United States of America

10   9   8   7   6   5   4   3   2   1

Library of Congress Cataloging-in-Publication Data

Frank, Milo O., date
    How to run a successful meeting—in half the time / Milo O.
    Frank.
        p.   cm.
    1. Business communication.   2. Meetings.   I. Title.
HF5718.F743   1989
658.4'56—dc20   89-8425
                                                               CIP

ISBN 0-671-64470-X

ACKNOWLEDGMENTS

Thank you to Sydney Swire, without whom this book might not be what it might be. To Laura Kelly for her endless hours and adept handling. To Joel Marks, who was there at the beginning.

And to Jim Lindberg, Phil Quigley, Arthur Gilbert, William Arnold III, Katie Boyd, Kurt Hirsch, Henri Temianka, Dick Carlson, Bill Williams, Anthony La Scala, Larry Kitchen, Ken Todd, Jeremy Tarcher, Hal Gershowitz, George Deukmajian, John Trajanski, Bill Brett, Charlie and Susan Floyd, Bill Maier, Bert and Jane Boeckmann, Nate Kates, Ed Kushell, Jack Black, Michael Feeney, Bill Woods, Lloyd Dennis, Dan Tellep, Bill Henry, Morley Benjamin, Bill Brock, Lady Mary Fairfax, Howard Wilkins, Anne Collins, Joe Manion, Pete Wilson, Leo Goodstadt, Roger

ACKNOWLEDGMENTS
_____

Gadd, Stephen Marcus, and John Sculley for their thoughts and anecdotes.

And a double thank you to Artie and Richard Pine, my esteemed agents, and Fred Hills and Burton Beals, my editors extraordinaires.

6

To my wife, Sally—
A DEDICATION
WITH DEDICATION

CONTENTS

Contents

INTRODUCTION

The Time of Your Life

Why didn't Russian soldiers have bulletproof vests in 1917?

My grandfather, an American businessman, designed and manufactured a type of legging used by our soldiers in the First World War. It seems the Russian General Staff was interested in acquiring bulletproof vests for its army, and he was asked to make a proposal. After thorough investigation he found he could convert his legging factory and manufacture and deliver the vests for three dollars each. This, even during the latter part of World War I, was an incredible bargain. The Russians called him to meeting after meeting—meetings on design and material, meetings on quality and quantity, meetings on guarantees and delivery dates, more meetings with generals, more meetings with colonels—days, weeks, and months of meetings.

Finally the Russians turned down the deal. "Why?" my grandfather asked. "These vests will save lives."

"Because," they said, "no Russian soldier's life is worth three dollars." That story became a part of our family history and was my first lesson about what a waste of time meetings can be.

Later in my career as a young motion picture agent, I was always trying to arrange meetings with the motion picture studios' senior executives in order to sell my clients. Our agency handled Humphrey Bogart, Marilyn Monroe, and many more stars, but that was later. At the beginning it was hard for me to get in to see heads of studios. I wanted a meeting with Steve Trilling, a senior executive who ran Warner Brothers for Jack Warner. It took me a month to arrange one. I waited in his outer office for thirty minutes. Then, finally, I was ushered in. As I began to speak I heard bells ringing in the distance, and then his phone rang. He answered, got up, and rushed out of his office—he never came back. There was a fire on one of the sound stages.

It took me another month to reschedule the meeting. This time Trilling kept me waiting forty-five minutes. Then I was brought in, seated, and offered a cup of coffee. As I began to speak I heard bells ringing in the distance, and then his phone rang—I still can't believe it. Trilling rushed out to the second fire on a sound stage in over twenty years at Warner Brothers Studio.

Those were the only two meetings I can recall that I wished were longer.

I now work as a consultant and lecturer in communication skills, strategies, and media training with the top executives and managers of many major corporations; the members of many associations, church groups, and charity organizations; and politicians from county supervisors to senators to candidates for the presidency of the United States. Over the years my work has involved literally thousands of meetings. Many of them were time wasters, and certainly most took twice as long as necessary. My experience is not unique. A recent nationwide survey of top executives reported in *The Wall Street Journal* revealed that meetings accounted for the greatest amount of their unproductive time, topping telephone calls, paperwork, travel, and office gossip.

But whether it's a one-on-one conversation with your boss or co-worker, or a gathering of five, ten, or twenty people in a conference room, meetings are a fact of our everyday business lives. When you stop to think about it, how well you present yourself and your ideas and how well you work with other people are the two basic essentials of any career. And that's exactly what meetings are all about. They are an important management tool. And the way you conduct yourself at meetings, whether as the leader or as a participant, can make or break your career.

Why, then, are so many meetings boring, unproductive—and almost always too long? Here are a few of the reasons:

- No specific, clear-cut "objective" for the meeting, its leaders, or its participants.
- No meeting agenda.
- Too many or the wrong choice of participants.
- No consideration for allies or antagonists.
- Failure to prepare properly.
- Inability to present ideas concisely.
- Lack of sound leadership and control.
- Improper use of visual aids.
- Too many digressions and interruptions.
- Time wasted on "why" rather than "how."
- Mixed final decisions.

Meetings don't have to be long and unproductive. There's another way. By mastering a few shortcuts and strategies you can get the job done—and in half the time. That's what this book is all about. You'll learn how to determine whether a meeting is really necessary (and how to say no if it isn't), how to prepare for a meeting, how to present your ideas concisely (and briefly), how to keep a meeting on track and on time, and much, much more.

This isn't a book that will tell you everything there is to know about meetings. This is a book of specific techniques and practical strategies that you can apply immediately—before, during, and after every meeting you attend. They are easy to learn. They are easy to use. They work.

ONE

To Meet or Not to Meet?

Q: When should you call a meeting?
A: When a meeting is the best way to achieve your objective.

FIRST STAR I SEE TONIGHT

When I was head of talent and casting for the CBS network, we started a new television show called *Best of Broadway*. Those were the early days of television when many of the stars we wanted were reluctant to appear. But I was able to get Claudette

Colbert (her TV debut), Helen Hayes, Fredric March, Nancy Olson, and Charles Coburn in the cast for one particular show. At that time it was the best "name" cast ever assembled on TV for a dramatic show, and was I proud—except I was in trouble. March, Hayes, and Colbert all wanted top billing or they would withdraw. The name that comes first on the marquee or screen is practically a matter of life and death to an actor, sometimes even more important than money.

I knew I was dealing with emotional temperaments. What were the alternatives? I began to ask myself questions like "If I lose Hayes, March, and Colbert in her TV debut, now after all the hullabaloo, will my popularity and my bonus become memories?" Then I became more practical and started to ask the right questions. "Is half a cake better than none? Is a third of the cake better?" I had it.

I called a meeting of the three agents involved. (Actually there were five, as two brought reinforcements.) In the meeting I told the agents that our play was in three acts. I suggested that, in order to make everybody happy, we give one of the actors top billing at the opening of the first act, one top billing at the opening of the second act, and the last top billing at the opening of the third act. That way everyone was served and no commissions would be lost.

"What about the crawl at the end of the show?" someone asked.

"Why, alphabetically, of course," I said calmly (quivering inwardly)—and that was that. As I remember, Helen Hayes's name was in the first position at the opening, Claudette Colbert came first in the middle, and Fredric March was first at the third act.

I wanted to keep all three of these stars on the show. That was my objective. But was a meeting the best way to achieve it? I considered my alternatives. I could have telephoned each agent separately. I could have written a note to each one. But it always came back to a meeting. A meeting with all three together would put the pressure on. What we agreed together would hold. That meeting was the *best* way to achieve my objective.

Q: What is your objective, and how do you find it?

A: Look for the goal, the purpose, the basic reason for holding a meeting.

DESTINATION MOON

A meeting without a clear-cut objective is a trip to nowhere. A trip to nowhere goes on forever.

23

In the early days of NASA, members held meetings with a clear-cut objective: land a man on the moon in ten years. They did. Since then, progress has been more difficult because of a lack of defined goals.

From middle managers to top executives, from assemblymen to senators to presidents, from lawyers to heads of universities and hospitals, I have found that few people really recognize the objectives of the meetings they call or are asked to attend. Quite simply, it is the purpose, the goal, the basic *reason* these meetings are being held. A single clear-cut objective is a great timesaver for any meeting. You know exactly why you are there and what you expect to accomplish.

Here are some typical meeting objectives:

- A casting director wants to keep three stars on a show.
- A corporation wants to improve product quality.
- A neighborhood association wants to build a playground.
- A family wants to buy a house.
- A man wants a job promotion.
- A corporation wants to sell a new stock issue.
- A department manager wants to sell an idea to management.
- A company wants to sell its services.
- A manager wants to hire additional help.
- A PTA wants to determine its goals for the year.

- A woman wants to get a job.
- A citizens' group wants to promote recycling.
- A company wants to improve its image.

Before you call or attend any meeting, make sure you know the objective of that meeting.

GOAL MINING

To find your objective, ask yourself:

- Why am *I* holding the meeting?
- Why am *I* going to participate in the meeting?
- What do *I* want to achieve at the meeting?
- What do *I* want to achieve after the meeting is over?

A meeting without a specific objective is almost certain to achieve nothing specific. And that's a waste of time.

Q: How do you know if your objective is best served by a meeting?
A: Look at the alternatives.

IS THIS MEETING REALLY NECESSARY?

Ask yourself the following questions to determine if you should hold a meeting:

1. Is a meeting the *only* means of fulfilling my objective?
2. If not, what are the alternatives?
3. How effective are the alternatives?
4. Is a meeting the *best* means of fulfilling my objective?
5. Will a meeting use my time and my colleagues' time to our best advantage (taking into account the time it will take to prepare for the meeting and the necessary follow-up meetings)?

AT&T was preparing a presentation and testimony for a Public Utilities Commission hearing. Many millions of dollars were at stake. I was called by the company, a client of mine, and asked to help in the strategy and preparation of the speeches and visual aids. There was to be a one-day rehearsal meeting and, a week later, a one-day "dress" rehearsal meeting. I would fly in the night before each of the two rehearsal days, work the day of the rehearsal, and fly home that night. It was also requested that I fly in an extra day during the week preceding the dress rehearsal to make suggestions and changes in the written material. I questioned whether *this* contemplated special meeting was necessary.

As I would become the meeting leader that extra day, it was necessary for me to make a decision as to whether or not to hold that meeting. I knew my expenses and fee, plus the time of the executives and writers, for this extra day would add up to a rather large amount. I also knew we could be equally productive if I worked with the writers on the phone. We would go over the material, they would make changes and phone me back, and we would repeat the procedure until we were all in accord. Then at the dress rehearsal we could make any additional changes. The objective would be fulfilled. Therefore, an extra meeting would be superfluous and wasteful. I phoned and explained my position. AT&T agreed. We had four phone conversations, and an unnecessary meeting was avoided. Both AT&T and I accomplished our objective, and valuable time and money were saved.

HOW TO MAKE SURE

Once you have determined the value of having a meeting, look again at any alternatives. Perhaps you can achieve your objective by phone calls to some of

27

the potential participants, as I did. Perhaps you can ask for a written response to a memo you will send, then handle the problem yourself. Once the value of the best alternative is again studied, you can finally decide which of the two, the meeting or the alternative, is better. You can then act accordingly.

> **Q:** Should you hold meetings on a routine basis?
> **A:** Routine meetings are effective only as long as each one continues to fulfill your objective.

THE ROUTINE RITUAL

Meetings held on a routine basis—weekly, bimonthly, monthly—are generally tedious and wasteful. Often you are forced to find or create situations in order to have something to talk about. It is far better to wait until a current situation or problem requires a meeting—then call it.

General Jim Lindberg told me a story about his early "meeting" days in business:

"My immediate superior, at a large corporation where I worked for a number of years, prescheduled a meeting with his department heads for every Monday morning at eight A.M. His objective was to keep his departments up to date on what everyone was doing. These meetings were a ritual, and you'd better be there, and on time.

"Each department head felt that he or she had to provide useful information or they would look bad. Often they had nothing new to discuss, so they talked about things in their departments that had no bearing on other departments. Nothing was accomplished. The original objective for holding the meeting had disappeared. As the weeks and months went by, the meetings deteriorated into a waste of time and a joke among the staff. Finally one of the group who was willing to take early retirement, and with his colleagues' promised support, faced up to the boss. 'Sir,' he said, 'these meetings don't work. They cost you and us time and money. Your original objective is not being met.'

" 'Is that so?' said the boss

"After considerable discussion—mostly friendly— the original objective of the meeting, keeping everyone up to date, was reexamined. It was decided that a simple one-page status report, sent to the appropriate people when necessary, would do the job. It did. Morale improved, productivity increased, and time was saved."

To this day Jim Lindberg thinks long and hard

about his objective and his alternatives before he calls a meeting.

> **Q:** What damage can an unnecessary meeting do?
> **A:** It can destroy your objective.

THE FISH THAT GOT AWAY

A business manager friend of mine found an excellent investment opportunity at a marina near Los Angeles. He talked to a number of his clients about the investment, and I was included. We liked the deal and gave him authority to proceed. During his negotiations the price was upped. We told the business manager to go ahead anyway, but his junior partners wanted a meeting with all of us to discuss the problem. We said on the phone, "Don't waste time, just close the deal." But no, we had to have a meeting. Weeks passed before everyone was available. At the meeting we all agreed to go forward, just as we had agreed in our phone conversations. Nothing new was accomplished. However, because of the passage of time, the sellers had found another buyer who, incidentally, paid more than we would have. They closed the deal with him, and within one year the value of the property had doubled.

One of the worst bureaucratic rules in business is "When in doubt, call a meeting." In this case, an "unnecessary" meeting was not only unnecessary but counterproductive.

Q: When can you gain more from a meeting you
don't have than from one you do?
A: When you can save everyone time.

THANKS FOR NOT COMING

Katie Boyd is an elegant woman and a magical fund-raiser. She has an imagination, too, as you can see by her invitation to a fund-raising meeting.

Katie's "non-meeting" was a highly successful fund-raiser. There were no deductions from the contributions to pay for an expensive party. And everyone saved time.

In the business world, there are many people who

You Are Cordially Invited To
"A NO PARTY AT ALL"

THE LARGEST EVER HELD IN THE STATE
OF CALIFORNIA

Everyone Is Invited
A Fund-raising Non-event Benefiting
BOB NAYLOR FOR U.S. SENATE
TIME: At your convenience, on or before June 3rd
PLACE: The Place of your Dreams with your favorite people
PROMISE: There will be no rubber chicken!
There will be no boring speeches!

CONTRIBUTIONS: Depend on your **DREAM!**
If your **DREAM** is a stroll in the park,
Or a fireside dinner at home, your
Contribution may be whatever you so desire;

BUT
If your **DREAM** is a trip to "Gay Paree,"
or a ride on the "Orient Express,"
a Contribution matching your **DREAM** will fill the bill
Your contribution is multiply valuable, as the only cost
of this non-party is the cost of this letter.
Dress Optional   Reservations Not Limited

think that holding or attending a continuous string of meetings is a sign of their power and importance. The exact opposite is true. If meetings are merely routine or unnecessary, they are a sure sign of bad management.

TWO

When You Call a Meeting

> **Q:** Who should participate?
> **A:** Those who can influence the fulfillment of the meeting objective.

THE GUEST LIST

Once upon a time a baby girl was born to a king and queen. In their joy, the royal couple invited the three good fairies of their kingdom to bestow magical gifts upon the tiny princess. Meeting at her cradle, the first fairy blessed the infant with incomparable beauty. The second fairy promised that the child would grow up to be as wise and good as she was beautiful. But before the third good fairy could present her gift, the evil witch Malevolent burst into the nursery. Furious at not having been invited to this event, she swore that when the child reached her sixteenth birthday, she would prick her finger upon a spinning wheel and die.

Fortunately the third fairy could countermand this evil curse. She decreed that the princess would prick her finger but instead of dying would sleep for one hundred years, until Prince Charming should awaken her with love's first kiss.

And so it happened, producing the longest postponement of any meeting on record—116 years before Sleeping Beauty and her prince could finally get together—and proving that you must be very careful indeed whom you invite or don't invite to your meetings.

Unnecessary participants, like unnecessary meetings, are of course a waste of everyone's time. Recognizing every participant's interests and objectives will lead to respect and friendship, which, in turn, leads to better results and shorter meetings. Most important, analyze the potential participants' feelings on the issue in question.

A person opposing your objective may do you more harm by being excluded from a meeting than by being present. The witch Malevolent is proof of that pudding. Often you can defuse any possible hostility by including the opponent in your discussion and showing respect for his position, however much you disagree. And of course you can always create a balance by inviting participants favorable to your cause. Most important, you will save time by avoiding hostility, which may lead to the undermining of your objective.

Ask yourself the following questions to help you decide whom to include.

1. Whom are you obligated to invite?
2. Who can give you what you want?
3. Who is in favor of your objective?
4. Who will oppose your objective?
5. Who is on the fence?
6. Who can cause trouble if not invited?

Q: How many participants should you include?
A: The number of people you invite is directly proportional to the length of any meeting.

THE FEWER THE MERRIER

A successful meeting depends on who is present. And who is present depends on who is invited.

When my wife and I attend large parties, we usually find that no matter how well planned the affair, there is little opportunity to really get to know and enjoy the company of the other guests. When we give a dinner party, we like to invite no more than four to six people. For us, six including ourselves is an ideal number. There is an opportunity for everyone to get to know each other and talk about interests they may have in common. Through the years this has resulted in many long-lasting friendships.

Business meetings are very similar: the more participants, the more difficult it is to achieve your objective. Sometimes company policy predetermines who will attend a meeting. But the more specific the objective of the meeting, the fewer the necessary participants. Here's where the psychology of group dynamics comes into play. Small groups invite candor, intimacy, and real results. When the group is larger than about ten people, the theatrics begin as opposing parties try to impress their colleagues, playing more for effect than for results.

Remember, no one will feel excluded or overlooked if he is excluded from a meeting with an objective in which he has no particular concern. In fact, he may thank you for *not* asking him to attend.

Q: How should you prepare?
A: Use the memo or agenda as both a blueprint and a plan of action for every meeting.

A STITCH IN TIME

One of the top five hundred companies in America had a real problem. Their marketing department was under fire for questionable market practices. Serious allegations were involved that were destroying the company's marketing image both internally and externally. The senior executive in charge of marketing, Steven, knew his days were numbered unless he was able to get some positive results. He planned a meeting.

Steven knew his objective: he had to reestablish his leadership in the department and eliminate the questionable marketing practice. He decided his four vice presidents best filled the requirements for achieving his objective. Other participants would only confuse the issue. He knew if he could firmly establish his control over those four people, it would carry down through the rest of the department. But he also knew that he had to advise and structure a plan that would lead to the fulfillment of his objective—*before* the meeting. And he had to focus the attention of all the participants on the issues to be discussed and inform them of what would be expected of them when they did meet. Unfocused exploratory meetings are like trying to find your way out of a labyrinth in the dark. A carefully prepared memo or agenda is the best way to save time and get results.

QUESTIONS CAN BE MORE CREATIVE THAN ANSWERS

Asking yourself the right questions will always help you find, formulate, and focus your ideas. Questions make you think. Sometimes they motivate you into coming up with new and imaginative ideas. To focus his own ideas as well as clarify the issues that would be discussed at the meeting, Steven asked himself the following questions about his department's marketing practices:

1. How did we do this in the past?
2. How effective was it?
3. How do we do it now?
4. How effective is it?
5. How might we do it in the future?

39

6. How effective might that be?

Steven formed the answers to those questions in his own mind. Now he wanted his four vice presidents to do the same—before they met—so he prepared a memo that became the blueprint for the meeting.

THE BLUEPRINT

Here's the memo he sent out:

In order for this department to continue in operation, we must eliminate questionable marketing practices and prepare a new coordinated marketing plan. Therefore, I would like each of you to develop (please, do not compare approaches) what you feel to be:

1. The three most important actions marketing needs to take to resolve the trust and confidence of our customers.
2. The three most important actions we must take internally to reverse the bad image marketing has acquired in the eyes of the rest of the company.

Please send these "action" plans in writing to me by next Tuesday. And please limit each of your six plans to one paragraph. I will discuss each action plan with you individually on the phone.

One week from next Tuesday, we will meet from two to three o'clock. Please be prepared to present your action plans as briefly and concisely as possible. We will then discuss them and decide which plans to put into effect.

The procedures as outlined were followed. The meeting was held, and the four vice presidents presented their plans. After discussion, those plans that were considered to be most effective were decided upon and implemented. Marketing was back on track, and Steven reestablished his control. All in one meeting of less than forty-five minutes. And all because of proper preparation.

SHORTER IS SWEETER

A written memo or agenda is the best means of giving and securing information and if properly put together will focus you as well as the recipients on the objective of the meeting and the means to achieve it. During the meeting it can also be used as a guide and reference, and after the meeting it can serve as a reminder of what was to be accomplished and a means of checking on follow-up actions. Time spent preparing a written memo or agenda will *save* time during any meeting. But keep it short. *Write no memo longer than one page.* Any additional materials, charts, or graphs necessary for the meeting should be included on separate pages, stapled or paper-clipped to your one-page memo.

Q: What should a good memo or agenda include?

A: It should state the objective of the meeting, the issues to be discussed, the time the meeting will begin *and* end, the place, the participants involved, and what is expected of them in the way of preparation before the meeting.

POOR MEMO POOR RESULT

A sports club meeting that a friend of mine attended recently carried a lot of lessons. The lessons began when he first received a note from the management committee chairman: "There will be a meeting of the management committee April 12th at 5 o'clock. RSVP please." That was it.

When the majority of the committee members arrived at the meeting, the chairman held up a large sheet of paper and asked if anyone had "happened" to see it. Of course no one had because it had not been previously available. The chairman then handed out the following paper to all present:

Items for Discussion
(All Suggestions of Members)

1. Pool: purchase new heater and automatic pool cover.
2. New dishes needed—ask Deirdre.
3. Paint club exterior.
4. Repaint game room + new carpets + recover furniture.
5. Resurface north side of patio.
6. Washer/dryer near locker area—where?
7. New scale in men's locker area—repaint ladies' and use it.
8. Replace locker name tags.
9. Wood paneling in sauna.
10. Plant high bushes beyond north fence (court #4).
11. Rowing machine? If so, put it where?

12. Garbage compactor.
13. Canopy or awning stretching south from dining room.
14. New umbrellas for patio tables.
15. New sinks in men's locker area.
16. Cover over air-conditioning ducts in men's locker room—vetoed by board on 4-12-87.
17. Cover pipes on ground at south end of court #8.
18. Solve parking problem—buy adjacent property?
    build parking structure?
    buy part of parking facility at corner?
    wait and see?

The meeting took—and wasted—an hour and a half. Nothing was accomplished. No specific actions were taken on any of the eighteen items. Here is why.

The memo the participants received in the mail told them nothing except that there would be a meeting. Only when they got there were they informed about the topics to be discussed. And even then they didn't know why. The members of the committee didn't have any time to research or look into each topic—other than at the meeting—in order to find out what the problems were and how to solve them. In short, neither the chairman nor the committee members were properly prepared, and another meeting had to be called. This time the committee chairman did his homework and gave the members of the committee time to do theirs.

FIRST THE MEMO

Here is the memo the committee chairman prepared and sent to members in advance of the next meeting:

To the Members of Management Committee:

Do you want to be a hero or a villain? Our fellow members have recently suggested a number of actions to be taken by the club. It is the job of the management committee, you, to approve or disapprove these suggestions. Please read carefully the attached suggestions. If you have special knowledge or are willing to research and obtain estimates on any of the listed items, please call me by 14 July. Those items on which I receive no call will be assigned committee members at my discretion.

There will be a meeting from 4:30 P.M. to 6:00 P.M. on 28 July for discussion and decision.

Each member will present the three best reasons to vote yes and the three best reasons to vote no on each item he has researched and his conclusion. Four minutes will be allowed on each item. Four additional minutes will be allowed for discussion by all committee members on each item. Two minutes will be allowed for vote on each item.

> Thank you,
> Committee Chairman

Attached separate sheet:
  Items for Discussion.

The following list of much more specific topics for discussion was attached to the memo:

Items for Discussion

1. Is a new pool heater purchase necessary? If so, where best location?
2. Should purchase of new dishes as recommended by manager (Deirdre) be approved?
3. Should exterior of club be painted? What color? And within what period of time?
4. Should game room be repainted? What color? Should we replace carpet? Whether room is painted or not? Should we recover furniture in either case?
5. Should the north side of the patio be resurfaced?
6. Should our washer/dryer be repaired or should we purchase a new one? Where should it be placed?

7. Should all locker name tags be replaced with uniform standard tags?
8. Should we purchase a new garbage compactor?

The memo, with items for discussion attached, was sent to each member of the committee two weeks prior to the meeting. The meeting was held as planned.

The results were phenomenal. Seven items got firm decisions. One was put in abeyance, to be decided upon by the board. All was accomplished within the circumscribed time limits. What made this possible was not just the proper preparation before the meeting, but also the actions taken during the meeting. First of all, the chairman was fully informed on all the topics for discussion, and he remained in control of the meeting. Second, the members came to the meeting fully prepared for their part in the discussion. The time limits set for the discussion of each item were strictly adhered to, and knowledgeable decisions could be made.

Careful preparation is the best way to keep any meeting on target and on time. It will cut your meeting time in half.

Q: Memo or menu: Should you mix meetings with meals?

A: Yes, if your objective is to establish a social as well as a business relationship.

JOURNEY TO THE STARS

As a young motion picture agent I had numerous luncheon meetings at Romanoff's, the great Beverly Hills restaurant in the days before the star system and movie studios joined Atlantis beneath the sea. I admit that sometimes my attention wandered from the meetings to the many stars who lunched there. But my star gazing was business-oriented because I wanted those actors as clients and used every opportunity to make that happen. Arranging appointments with prospective clients while dining at star-studded restaurants paid off for me. Naturally each such luncheon took twice as long as it should have, but in the long run it was worth it in time saved. Countless wasted telephone calls to principals and second and third parties to try to arrange a meeting were avoided. Meetings with a principal's agent, which almost never led to a meeting with the principal, were unnecessary.

The social approach to achieve your business objective is a powerful tool. With my business objective in mind, I have arranged social evenings where the word *business* was not even mentioned. But it is always best if you conclude the social meeting by setting a date for a business meeting in a business setting. Because the ice has already been broken, and the beginning of a relationship put in motion, your business meeting will be shorter and more effective.

If, on the other hand, you must use a meal meeting strictly for business, with a minimum of social overtones, you can often get better results and save time depending on which meal you choose— breakfast, lunch, or dinner.

BREAKFAST IS BEST

Godfrey Sperling, Jr., senior Washington columnist for the *Christian Science Monitor*, is famous for the breakfast meetings he hosts. At these meetings political figures are interviewed by invited members of the press over scrambled eggs and orange juice. When these culinary press conferences were initiated, the early morning meeting time was considered unusual. The choice was deliberate. As a Christian Scientist, Sperling doesn't drink and did not wish to provide liquor at the press conferences. It works for him in more than one way. Not only are the guests of honor more likely to be available for interviews at an early hour, but less time is wasted on socializing or eating an elaborate meal.

The so-called power breakfast has come to be the rule rather than the exception for the motion picture and television business.

But no one comes to a power breakfast to eat. They come to meet and to greet. Breakfast meetings have several advantages. You may feel fresher in the morning, and since you have to eat anyway, why not use the time productively, perhaps even arrange a future meeting on the spot that otherwise might not happen? Some executives are not famous for returning phone calls; face to face, they are stuck and will make an appointment. And breakfast meetings are usually short. When breakfast is over, so, ostensibly, is the meeting. Everyone has something else to do.

HOW TO HEAR THE ROOSTER CROW

Kurt Hirsch is a meeting man. How else can you become one of the top insurance salesmen in America? And on more than one occasion he has resorted to his own version of the power breakfast. This is the story he told me:

"Through the recommendation of an existing client, I was referred to the owner of a large garment manufacturing business in connection with his employee group medical plan. But several meetings with this gentleman and his controller proved less than satisfactory because of incessant interruptions from department store buyers, his staff, and a never-ending succession of telephone calls.

"I remembered that executives in the garment business worry a lot and keep very early hours. So finally, after the umpteenth interruption, I got up, closed my briefcase, and asked the owner what time he usually arrived at his office. 'Five A.M.,' he replied.

" 'Could I have a meeting with you tomorrow or the following day at five A.M.?' I asked him. His controller gave me a peculiar look, but the owner agreed to a five A.M. appointment the following week.

"It is practical to remember that at five A.M. the telephones are asleep, too. When I arrived for our meeting, I brought some bagels, cream cheese, lox, and a Thermos of coffee with me. The meeting took place under the most favorable of circumstances, and a few weeks later I closed this prestigious and financially lucrative deal.

"Sometime later I asked my new client why he had elected to do business with me, knowing that my bid was not the lowest of those submitted. His reply was short and to the point. I got the deal because I was willing to go downtown and meet with him on his terms—his office at five A.M. He had apparently had similar conversations with other brokers who obviously were not, and even more important, I was fifteen minutes early and finished by 5:15 A.M. before any interruptions. He said I made a potentially long meeting short by planning the best time to meet. That reflected to him a timesaving relationship. After all, I brought breakfast, which showed I was thought-ful of him *and* I saved him another hour later when he would have gone out to eat. And what could be more important?"

Breakfast at the Waldorf couldn't have gotten a better result for Kurt Hirsch than the few dollars he spent on bagels, lox, and coffee—and the Waldorf dining room wasn't open anyway.

LUNCHEON IS LONGER

Luncheon meetings are another matter. They always take longer, and there is always time taken for a cocktail, even if it is a plain Perrier masking as a highball.

Henri Temianka, concert violinist and founder and conductor of the California Chamber Symphony, has warned of the dangers of the luncheon-hour meeting:

It would seem that a normal lunch meeting
Consists mostly of boozing and greeting.
At the session's late start
The well-fed depart
With the late-comers still busy eating.

I have three rules to shorten luncheon meetings and achieve better results:

1. Pick a restaurant closest to a majority of those attending—less travel time required.
2. Come early—better service, and out faster.
3. Limit alcohol—it shortens the attention span and lengthens the meeting.

THE WINNER IS . . .

Sybil Brand holds three meetings a week and has done so for years. A fantastic woman, she is chairman of the Institutional Inspection Commission for the county of Los Angeles. She has very few luncheon meetings. She learned the hard way.

I was on the Los Angeles County Institutional Inspection Commission with Sybil for seven years. Occasionally we had to attend luncheon meetings at some of the institutions we visited. We dreaded those meetings because whenever there were thirty people or more attending—and there usually were more—each person would be introduced by name and title with a few complimentary words added. The person would then stand and say, "Thank you," and in some cases a lot more. It was like the

Academy Awards. Needless to say, this added an hour to the already too long meeting.

If you want to shorten any meeting, do not introduce anyone except those participants who are directly involved in the objectives of the meeting.

AT DINNER YOU'RE DIMMER

Dinner meetings can be the best or the worst: the best for the social approach and the worst for specific business objectives. You're tired; one just does not think clearly at the end of a busy day. It's like jet lag. Everyone thinks he is thinking clearly, but he is not. Some Australian companies I work with have a strict business rule. When their people come to the United States to do business, they are not allowed to consummate a deal until at least forty-eight hours have passed, the minimum time required to recover from their jet lag. Slow thinking makes slow meetings.

If you must have a dinner meeting, begin early and finish early. And I might note that the better and more elegant the restaurant, the longer your meeting and the harder it is to achieve your objective. When you're spending a small fortune for dinner, you certainly don't hurry the evening. After all, nobody is hurrying to pay the national debt, either.

THREE

When You Attend a Meeting

Q: When should you attend a meeting that you
   think will be a waste of time?
A: When a meeting avoided is an opportunity
   wasted.

LOOK FOR THE SILVER LINING

If there is a meeting you should attend and you are
invited, attend. If you are not invited and it is
important, then find a way to get invited. But what
about those time-wasting meetings that you cannot

control and must attend, no matter how much they seem like time out of your life? Then bite the bullet and go, but treat it as career training, not business. Determine how the meeting can be of value to you, and learn all you can about the leader and the other participants. Recognize that every meeting is an opportunity to fulfill your personal objective.

Q: What preparation is required to make any meeting work for you?

A: A brief prepared message is essential to every participant in every meeting.

DON'T BE A WALLFLOWER

I was once in a round-table discussion meeting on television. There were six of us at the table. The subject was health, business, and communications. There was a host moderator, and it was basically a question-and-answer situation. I hadn't wanted to be there because of prior commitments, but a doctor friend had asked me and I couldn't refuse him.

Just before I went in to the meeting, I had seen a headline on the back section of the newspaper lying on a table in the anteroom. It read UGLY DOGS DIE. I scanned it quickly. It was about two puppies that had been brought to the pound and, because they were ugly—even though the owner had made a small donation—were put to death in two hours. I decided I would do something about that unfortunate situation. I would make what could have been a waste of time for me a valuable opportunity. It was too late for the puppies, but I would use this meeting about health, business, and communications to find a home for some needy animals. I prepared my message. It only took me a few minutes—actually, less than five. I knew the subject would never be brought up, as it had nothing to do with any of the preset meeting issues. At the most appropriate point I would create my opportunity. It was easy. Someone asked about the most important techniques in communicating. I said, "One of the most important is attracting your listener's attention. While I was waiting outside, I read a headline, UGLY DOGS DIE. That really grabbed my attention. I had to read the article."

I had the floor, control, and everyone's attention. I told them briefly of the incident I had read about in the article and then said to the TV viewers as well as those present, "Go to the pound and save a doomed animal. It will make you feel good, it will save a life, and it is a known medical fact"—I was able to bring in health, one of our issues—"that people with pets live longer."

The reaction was excellent. Everyone at the meeting was nodding, and I don't mean going to sleep. No one had the faintest conception that I had planned the message. It did not disturb the meeting. It took no longer than forty-five seconds, including answering the question, and it allowed me to achieve my objective.

Just answering other people's questions or keeping quiet will not take advantage of a meeting opportunity. First you must develop a concise message, then find or create an opportunity in the meeting to get that message across. You will command understanding and respect because a brief statement can work in a busy meeting where a "dissertation" would be cut off or relegated to another time and place.

Q: Is there a specific form for your concise message?

A: Every message should include a "grabber" opening, a main idea, and a demand on the audience.

1-2-3

A manager working for Chemical Waste Management, a subsidiary of Waste Management, Inc., the

largest and certainly one of the best waste-disposal
companies in America, was asked to attend a meeting
with a group of young people who were adversarial
and claimed that Chemical Waste Management was
hurting the environment. The manager was invited
to the meeting not as a presenter, but merely as a
participant. He knew that he should not waste an
opportunity by just sitting and listening or becoming
a target for adversarial questions. He knew that
defensive answers are like the Maginot Line; they
don't win friends or wars. He decided to create an
opportunity to disarm the adversaries of his company. To that end, he prepared this brief message:

Grabber Opening: The Sunday *New York
                        Times,* one of our
                        greatest newspapers,
                        costs 75,000 trees. The
                        Sunday *Chicago
                        Tribune* costs 16,500
                        trees. We had better
                        take pictures of our
                        forests so our
Main Idea: grandchildren will
                        know what a tree
                        looked like. Or better
                        still, recycle and save
                        the trees, and then *their*

	children can even climb them. My company is a leading proponent of recycling, and
Demand on Audience:	we want you to get involved. You can write or call me and we can talk about how what we do benefits us all.

The Chemical Waste manager was now prepared for the meeting. He had a structure that made his message coherent, relevant, and concise.

> **Q:** How can you be sure you don't forget an important point in your message?
> **A:** Use notes.

HOW TO PREPARE YOUR NOTES AND VICE VERSA

It was only when I began to write screenplays and dialogue that I realized the written word, the narrative form, was not appropriate to speaking situations. Even in the hands or mouths of experts it becomes stilted. Dialogue is people talking to each other. How do you create dialogue that is generally conversational? Easy. You do it every day when you talk to somebody about a subject that moves you emotionally or about which you have strong feelings. So first, write out exactly what you want to say. Then, take a three-by-five card and, holding it vertically, make your notes in as few words as possible. Here's what the Chemical Waste manager's notes looked like:

Notes	Talk
Times 75,000	The Sunday New York Times, one of our greatest newspapers, costs 75,000 trees.
Trib 16,500	The Sunday Chicago Tribune costs 16,500 trees. We had better take pictures of
Grandchildren	our forests so our grandchildren will know what a tree looked like. Or better still, recycle and save the trees, and
Climb	then their children can even climb them.

Recycle	My company is a leading proponent of recycling, and we want you to get involved.
Call	You can write or call me and we can talk about how what we do benefits us all.

During the meeting, the Chemical Waste manager found an opportunity to deliver his brief message—and with his notes on the three-by-five card in the palm of his hand, he was able to include everything he wanted to say without reading it like a speech. He made his point.

Q: How do you prepare for a meeting where there is opposition to your objective?

A: Determine your opponent's objective before the meeting.

DIFFERING GOALS

During the McCarthy era and the communist witch hunt throughout the entertainment industry, I was head of talent and casting for CBS television. At the time, CBS had more in-house shows than all the other networks and studios combined. These included *Suspense, Danger, Studio One, The Arthur Godfrey Show, The Ed Sullivan Show,* and so on. As head of talent I was responsible for casting every actor on every show.

CBS would not and did not knowingly hire communists, and before I cast any player, I had been instructed to call a special number at the network. I did not know whom I was calling. A male voice would answer. I would give him the name of the actor to be hired, and within twenty-four hours I would get a call-back telling me whether I could or could not hire the actor. This was a purely political procedure. At the time there were many pressures, and CBS had to be careful. We would get thousands of calls if an actor thought to be a communist went on the air. In one extreme case, the network was besieged with calls when a baby's crying, a voice-over by a woman who had been labeled a communist, was heard on the show. There was no name credit and no one knew how she had ever been identified.

With well-known stars for my shows, I would sometimes do the hiring first and *then* make the call. One day I hired Vincent Price. I phoned his name in and forgot about it. The next day I got the usual call-back. The voice said, "No on Vincent Price."

63

"What are you talking about?"

"No. Don't hire him," the voice replied.

"Well," I said, "it's too late. I've already hired him."

"Unhire him," said the voice.

"No," I said, "I know he's not a communist."

"We'll get back to you," the voice said.

That afternoon I got a call to come to a meeting and see the person, who until then had been only a voice. There were two people waiting for me. Their objective was to avoid political controversy for CBS by allowing no communists on the network. My objective was to keep Price on the show. It was a tough situation, and I knew my job might be on the line. They made their point that Price should be quietly let go and even paid, if necessary. I was prepared. I said, "Is Vincent Price really a communist? I know he isn't. I won't be a party to ruining his career on hearsay. If you want to fire him, you do it." And because I knew their objective—not to fire Price, but, basically, to avoid bad image-making publicity, I continued, "I will, of course, go to the newspapers."

"We'll get back to you," they said. They never did. Vincent Price went on the air. There were no repercussions, no calls or letters of protest, and everyone was happy. Some months later Vincent Price heard about the incident and gave me a painting. I still have it.

There is nothing wrong with your having an objective that is different from the objective of the leader of the meeting or the other participants. My knowledge of CBS's real objective helped me achieve mine. If you find yourself in a potentially adversarial situation, be prepared and be concise.

HOW TO DETERMINE AN OPPONENT'S OBJECTIVE

Ask yourself:

1. What does my opponent want?
2. Why does he want it?

HOW TO DETERMINE YOUR STRATEGY

Ask yourself:

1. What are the strongest points in *favor* of my opponent's objective?
2. What are the strongest points *against* it?
3. Who else is on my opponent's side?
4. Who are my allies?

5. What are the strongest points I can make that will accomplish my objective?

By the answers to these questions, you can measure your chances of success and plan your strategy accordingly. Otherwise it's guesswork.

Q: Is there a way to guarantee success for your objective in any meeting?

A: Getting the right people on your side *in advance* will save endless time and lost causes.

WHY A ROUND TABLE IS NOT AROUND

King Arthur's Round Table failed because he was unable to hold the alliances necessary to fulfill his objective of peace and unity throughout his kingdom. In the Arthurian legend of the Round Table, the conflict between Arthur, Lancelot, and Guinevere created factions that divided this great meeting place. Objectives became clouded, leadership faded, and King Arthur's cause fell into oblivion.

Meetings drag on endlessly and are often totally

wasteful because of a lack of shared objectives. Here is a true and perfect example, as it was described to me by a friend.

"At one of the largest publicly owned utilities in the United States, with a three-billion-dollar operating budget and nearly eleven thousand employees, senior officers of both human resources and management information systems had prepared respectively new program proposals for car pooling and a pilot electronic mail program. The research and development stages for each of these proposals had taken between four and six months, and much material, professional charts, and the like had been prepared. After extensive presentations, covering timeliness, costs both direct and indirect, and benefits to department heads and customers, the meeting participants were called upon for comment. Nearly everyone present at the meeting—between eight and ten other department heads—had suggestions for improvements and modifications. Why? Because they had not been given an opportunity to study the proposals in advance and, in most cases, were seeing them for the first time. Consequently, the discussion on these proposals alone took two or three times the allotted time for the entire meeting. So many changes were suggested by the other participants that the makers of the original proposals had to spend another six to eight months revising them. In that length of time people leave, conditions change, and good projects fall by the wayside, as these did."

BUY THEM IN—IN ADVANCE

Obviously, if the chairman of the meeting (the chief executive officer) had been consulted beforehand to help "bless" the projects, and other department heads, particularly the long-winded, reactive, and negative ones, had been briefed prior to the presentation to help buy them in, better results in a shorter period of time would have been achieved. My friend can attest to the effectiveness of this method because that's exactly what he did before his own later presentation. The result was so fast and easy that he had to hold himself back from suggesting that his proposal be further discussed before final acceptance.

ALLIANCES WIN WARS

Get alliance and support in advance. Even better, get approval before your meeting from the person or persons authorized to make a final decision. Well then, you might ask, why have the meeting? Use the meeting as an informational forum and a courtesy to all those who will be involved in the decision. And take advantage of any helpful suggestions that may be offered by the participants.

FOUR

The Meeting

> **Q:** What are the best tools for overcoming meeting pressures?
>
> **A:** Knowing what to say and how to say it.

THE PRESSURE COOKER

Meetings are pressure situations. If it's not time pressure, it's peer pressure. Everyone wants to look good in front of his associates. If it's not peer pressure, it's competition pressure. Everyone wants to look good in front of his boss. And let's not forget the pressure to make decisions. No decisions means wasted time and more meetings.

It is vital in any meeting to be able to say exactly what you want to say in an interesting manner and in as short a period of time as possible. You'll earn the respect of your peers and the boss, facilitate the decision-making process—and save time. And remember, somebody always has to get somewhere and others just want to go home.

> **Q:** Where should the leader sit?
> **A:** Where he will be the focus of attention.

KING OF THE MOUNTAIN

The placement of a king or queen's throne is not happenstance. It is deliberately placed above and slightly apart from the audience where it will be the focus of attention. By the same token, the leader of a meeting is, or should be, the focus of attention. Common sense dictates that he sit in the most visible spot. It is then easier for the participants to see and hear the leader and for him to see and hear them—and, of course, to control the meeting.

The end of a rectangular table farthest from the

entrance to the meeting room is the best place for the leader to sit. A leader could also sit in the center seat along the length of the table, but this and other positions do not command as much attention. If, for example, the leader sits next to the head of the table, he lends attention to the person sitting at the head and weakens his own authority. In the case of a round table, just visualize a long rectangular table in the room and sit where the head would be, farthest from the entrance to the room.

Q: Where should a participant sit?
A: Opposite the meeting leader, if possible.

FOR THE REST OF US BUMS

If you are an average participant, sit opposite the leader if you can. It allows you to talk directly to him and include the other participants as well. If you jockey to sit next to the leader, you may annoy the other participants—and the leader. On the other hand, do not sit as far away from him as possible, unless you are changing jobs and going to a competitor. How do you get the best seat in the room? Easy. Get there first.

Does where participants sit shorten the length of a meeting? It usually does, because clear lines of authority are established and the meeting is kept under control.

COMFORT IS GREAT—FOR INSOMNIA

Whether you are the meeting leader or a participant—and let me emphasize that every meeting participant becomes the meeting leader when it is his turn to speak—there are two "seating" points to remember.

First, recognize that wherever you sit, the comfort of the chair you are sitting on is inversely proportionate to your energy level, and your energy level is directly proportionate to the speed with which you achieve your objective.

Second, to overcome the nap-inducing characteristics of the few comfortable chairs you ever find in meetings, sit on the edge of your seat. This holds true not only for meetings, but for any interview, including radio and TV appearances. This position keeps you alert and adds energy. It makes you come across to your listener and/or viewer with more intensity

73

and power. It can also help you be a more involved and confident person, and that is a sure way to make friends and get better results.

> **Q:** Should you read your prepared message aloud?
>
> **A:** Yes, if you want your credibility to drop to zero.

READ IN BED

No presentation or statement, other than the Miranda rights, should ever be read aloud or, for that matter, memorized. Both these procedures make you subservient to your material. The material controls you rather than the reverse. Think about the way you chat with your family, with good friends, or with longtime business associates. You are natural and easy. You smile and gesture. You express warmth and feeling. All of these mannerisms or attitudes are the basics of excellent communicating.

> **Q:** How do you make someone else's question serve your purpose?
>
> **A:** Use it as a bridge to your own message.

CROSS THE BRIDGE TO YOUR DESTINATION

I am a participant in a meeting and I do not have the
floor. If I get a chance, I want to say, "Most meetings
are twice as long as they should be." In one of the
question-and-answer periods, somebody asks me,
"How long are most meetings?" It's a very easy
matter for me to answer, "Most meetings are twice as
long as they should be." I have gotten my message
across. But what if someone asks me, "What did you
have for breakfast?"

I think and answer, "Fresh fruit, cereal, sourdough
toast, jam, and coffee. A big breakfast. And I usually
need it because most of the meetings I attend are
twice as long as they should be, so I'm prepared if
we're late for lunch."

I was asked about breakfast and I told the ques-
tioner how long most meetings are. I answered his
question in the process. That is the technique of
making any question a bridge to your prepared
message.

TURNING MR. HYDE INTO DR. JEKYLL

Let's go back to our Chemical Waste Management
manager. He was sitting quietly in the meeting with

the adversary environmental group. He has not spoken and has not been addressed. But about halfway through the meeting a young woman said, "Waste is the right name for you. You people waste the environment. You're just in this game for the money, aren't you? You only care about the profit, don't you?"

There was the manager's opportunity. Even though the question was not put to him, he answered, "Every business tries to make a profit. That's how to stay in business. But we also spend money, too. To keep us all safe we continually change our procedures. We create new technology. Do you know that the Sunday *New York Times* costs 75,000 trees . . ." And he then delivered his prepared message.

The man from Chemical Waste got his message across perfectly. He only glanced once or twice at the three-by-five card, and no one even noticed. He was animated and spoke naturally because the few notes on the card forced him to make his point conversationally. He took a vicious adversary question and treated it as an opportunity. He answered the question, then made a smooth transition to his prepared message.

A question in any situation will also give you an opportunity to say what you want to say. It's a technique that's made for meetings. There are two absolute musts: Always answer the question, and always make your point. But even a question you don't know the answer to is an opportunity not to be wasted. If you don't know the answer, say, "I don't know. I'll find out and let you know. But something I do know . . ." and go on to make your statement. Or you can use the same technique in response to a statement. An individual at the meeting might have said, "The environment is our greatest asset." And the Chemical Waste Management manager could have said, "That is a powerful and true statement, and that's why we have to be aware of any change in that environment," and gone right into the rest of his message.

THE NAME OF THE GAME

I cannot emphasize enough that using someone else's question or statement to get a prepared, short message across is absolutely the best method of achieving your objective in any meeting. Moreover, the minute any participant answers a question and turns his answer into his prepared statement, he becomes the leader and controls the meeting while he is speaking. If the subject he introduces continues under discussion, his control continues as well.

A SHARP POINT STICKS

It has always amused me when in a trial a judge says, "Strike that last remark. Eliminate it from the record. The jury will disregard it." We all know that it is now firmly entrenched in the minds of the jury and everyone else. It has been emphasized by the lawyer when he demanded it be struck. It has been emphasized by the judge. It cannot be taken back. It is precisely like telling someone to think of anything in the world except elephants. They will then think of nothing but elephants. In the same fashion, when you use a question as an opportunity to make your point, it will stick in the mind of your listener.

Q: What is the single most powerful technique in communicating your message?
A: A personal story that makes your point.

YOURS TRULY

One of my clients is AT&T. I was working with operator services. Some of the operators were going out to a shopping center to meet with the public. Their objective was to get people to sign up or stay with AT&T. My job was to give them the skills and techniques to do this.

In a practice session I asked an operator by the name of Jane to pretend we were potential customers. She said, "We at AT&T are here to serve you. We have high-quality personnel and services, and we value our customers. We want to do the best job. Operators can make the difference. We are a high-technology company. We care . . ." and so on.

During her presentation, everyone was bored because she showed no energy. Her face had no animation or expression. Her tone was flat and her comments were dull. She had no real sincerity or belief. How could she? She was bored, too. She was giving out a "hype" message. The party line—and that's not meant as a pun. Try as she might, Jane was unable to get involved in her material.

During a break, I asked her if she'd had any interesting experiences lately. "Yes," she said. "One night about a month ago, I was on the line. I remember it was very late. I got a call. I couldn't understand what the man was saying. He sounded like a runner gasping for breath. I realized he was having a heart attack. I tracked him down. I got the paramedics. I saved his life.

"All the way home that night I thought to myself,

Thank God for operators who have our experience and training. I knew that if I had an emergency in my home, all I would have to do is call an operator. What a difference an operator really makes. That's the best reason I can think of for staying with us at AT&T."

That whole personal experience took less than thirty seconds to relate. And while telling her story Jane was a different person. Her face showed animation and expression. Her voice changed in tone and speed. Intensity of feeling, confidence, and belief were all there. And her sincerity was catching. How could it not be, since she was deeply involved in her own true experience? I asked Jane to repeat that story when we returned to the meeting. It had a dramatic effect on the other operators. And it was equally effective at the shopping center.

Under pressure it is sometimes hard to remember what you are going to say. Not when you tell personal stories. It is hard to forget your own experiences, and easier still to talk about them. It is also easy for people to identify with your personal stories. The more dramatic or humorous your personal story, the more effective it will be—but it must be true.

SEEING IN THE DARK

Spoken words are like smoke in the wind. They disappear quickly from the mind and memory.

Therefore you must make people see your spoken words as well as hear them. Word pictures stay in the minds of your listeners. They may forget the words themselves, but they'll remember visual imagery and identify with you and your objective. The sentence "Spoken words are like smoke in the wind" is a perfect example. It creates a picture in your mind. Telling personal stories is the best presentation technique because these stories almost always include word pictures.

Your objective at any meeting is to get your message across as effectively as possible. A vivid personal story will do that—and in much less time.

Q: What is often more important than the content of your message?
A: How you say it.

CHARM SCHOOL

Unfortunately, or perhaps fortunately, it's often not what we say but how we say it that makes the most lasting impression. Meetings are an arena in which people are selling their wares in every direction.

How we present ourselves often determines the success of our sale.

Before you attend any meeting you should have prepared what you are going to say. Here is *how* you should say it:

Techniques for Good Self-Presentation	How to Achieve Them
1. Expression and animation	Feel good and care about what you say.
2. Self-confidence and sincerity	Believe in what you say.
3. Appropriate body language and gestures	Relax and don't think about it.
4. Eye contact	Sight on your target.
5. Energy and enthusiasm	Like what you talk about.
6. Credibility	Speak the truth.
7. Emotion	Allow your feelings freedom.
8. Variations in the tone, level, and speed of your voice	Think of the variations a musician gets with his violin.

9. Smile	Think of what amuses you.
10. Personalization	Be yourself. Tell stories about yourself.

Practice in front of a mirror or in front of your husband or wife or a good friend. You are not born with the ability to communicate brilliantly. It is a learned process. And once you have learned it, you'll say what you want to say in half the time—and your audience will remember it.

> **Q:** What are the four elements that will make a meeting twice as successful in half the time?
> **A:** Time constraints, preparation, proper presentation, and control.

THE FOUR GRACES

When the Khmer Rouge, the Red Army, rolled over Cambodia, listening to international broadcasting was absolutely forbidden and punishable by death. Consequently thousands of people buried their radios in gardens, in backyards, and in the jungle. But in

1979, when the new regime seized power in Pnom-penh, it was once more possible, to a degree, to listen to the radio. Those encrusted radios were dug up out of gardens and schoolyards and fields around the country.

The Voice of America was the only broadcast that came from a free society. But what about new batteries for the radios? There were none for sale. The Kampucheans were so hungry for *The Voice of America* that they figured out how to reuse the old batteries. You could soak them in water, put them out on stones in the sun to dry, slap them back in the radio, and get, perhaps, another hour or so of uncensored world news from *The Voice of America*. The Kampucheans called the broadcasts a "breath of life."

Let's go to where this "breath of life" was born— Washington, D.C. The staff meetings of *The Voice of America* in Washington, D.C., take place at exactly 9:00 A.M., five days a week, every week. There are always twelve or more people present. As a result of the planning before these meetings and the actions taken at the meetings, more than 120 million people are able to turn on their radios and listen to *The Voice of America*, in spite of the fact that in some places listening means death.

So it would seem that when these twelve people meet to deal with issues ranging from weather and news to life and death to the fate of nations, it would require very long meetings—and until recently it did. The meetings ran hours. Now, because of proper planning, preparation, and control, although the meetings still start at 9:00 A.M., they finish at 9:15 A.M. sharp. Every 9:00 A.M., five days a week, each meeting takes fifteen minutes and that's it.

The four operative precepts that enable these meetings to be successful in far less than half the time required previously are

1. Time Constraints.

At 9:30 sharp every morning, five days a week, *The Voice of America* director, Dick Carlson, must be across the street for a meeting with the managers of the United States Information Agency. These meetings involve foreign policy and security and must be on schedule. This means *The Voice of America* 9:00 A.M. meeting *must* finish by 9:15 A.M.

2. Preparation.

The preplanning for every meeting is formalized. There is a written agenda. If any written response is required, it is limited in number of words. This agenda includes the specific issues and the clear-cut objectives to be addressed at each meeting. It also informs participants of what will be expected of them at the meeting, and provides a time limit for both participant and the subject under discussion.

3. Proper Presentation.

Each participant is expected to present his or her viewpoint in a clear, concise, and interesting manner within the prescribed length of time.

4. Control.

The director controls the meeting—and each person's participation. Priorities are set, and a firm but polite attitude prevails.

The Voice of America is still on the air—and expanding—so the results of these brief, but effective, meetings are obvious.

FIVE

Visuals, Props, and Calculated Risks

> **Q:** Why is a visual aid more concise than spoken words?
> **A:** Pictures are instantly comprehended; words are not.

INTER OR INTRA

In front of you is a map of the western part of the United States. The state of California is outlined in red. There is a large drawing of an airplane next to Los Angeles. The name of the airplane is on the plane. From Los Angeles, lines extend to eight or nine cities throughout the state. Since there are no lines drawn into the other states shown on the map, you know immediately, without any words spoken, where this airline flies, only inside the state of California.

However, if I were to say, "X Airline flies intrastate but not interstate," your mind would have to examine or decode the statement: Is interstate between states or within the state? While this thought process is taking place, you won't be able to concentrate on what is being said next. In short, the familiar cliché is usually true: one picture *is* worth a thousand words. If a visual aid will get your message across effectively, it is a big timesaver at any meeting.

Q: Should a visual aid be the most important aspect of your presentation?

A: A visual aid is just that—an aid to the speaker, not the main event.

WHO'S THE STAR?

It seems that every time I turn around I have to go to a meeting. And despite this vast expenditure of time and energy, I have rarely been impressed with the quality of the presentations to which I have been subjected.

I recently attended a meeting at a local hotel where thirty-five managers were wedged into the typical "classroom" configuration. Even from my vantage point halfway from the screen, I could not read the Vu-Graphs that one speaker continued to inflict upon us for an hour. Each Vu-Graph was no more than a copy of a typed page with about 250 words. Fortunately the room was dark enough for me to close my eyes. On another occasion, almost two hours passed before a break was called and we squirming attendees could flee to the restrooms. Don't speakers have bladders?

At meeting after meeting, the most frequent experience I encounter in visual presentations is a total lack of direction and pacing. Even a free-form brainstorming meeting needs direction and pacing. Wouldn't it be great if all visuals were intelligently planned, interesting, informative, memorable, human—and shorter?

This is what John Trajanski, a bright young staff manager, had to say about meetings. The opinions he expressed in his message to me are typical, and that is frightening. It is perhaps even more frightening to realize that although his concerns can be handled effectively, with specific techniques, almost no one seems to be aware that these techniques even exist.

IF YOU DON'T HAVE A BROKEN LEG

If you're considering using a visual aid or requesting that someone else use a visual aid as part of his or her presentation, please realize that *any* visual aid should be used to *complement* the speaker's presentation, not cause the listener or viewer to divide his attention between the two. Visuals, particularly Vu-Graphs and slides, are often used as crutches. They are also habit forming. They take the place of notes, and the presenter counts on them to keep him on track. They control him rather than the other way around.

SEE, HEAR, OR BOTH

Here are some simple questions to ask yourself in order to determine whether or not to prepare and use Vu-Graphs, slides, tapes, or charts:

1. Is the meeting room conducive to visuals?

2. Are my visuals better than the proverbial thousand words?
3. What kind of visual is best to reinforce a particular point?
4. Is it illustrative of my words?
5. Is my visual truly visual, or is it a photograph of a lot of words?
6. In each instance does it illustrate clearly the point I wish to make?
7. Are the visuals repetitive?
8. Will they save time and hold the audience's attention or just the reverse?

Q: How do you save time in the use of flip charts, Vu-Graphs, and slides?

A: Vivid images, careful preparation, concise presentation, and silence during viewing are the keys.

HANDLE WITH CARE

Visual aids are props. If they are dull or misused, they can ruin a presentation. If they are used properly, they can shorten a meeting and make it more productive.

HOW TO USE A FLIP CHART

A flip chart, like the old-fashioned blackboard, can be used to emphasize the main points of your message. Because they must be read, flip charts are obviously more effective with small groups. Here are some tips to remember:

1. Position the flip chart in a corner of room, not the center.
2. Ask if everyone can see. Adjust the chart accordingly.
3. If the charts have been prepared in advance, you can simply turn the pages without pause. But if you are writing on them as you go along, do not speak as you are writing.
4. Print.
5. When you speak, face the audience.
6. When you turn to the chart to indicate something, do not speak again until you turn back to your listeners. Consider the chart your silent friend reinforcing your spoken words.
7. Write only key words or short abbreviated sen-

tences. Keep less than twenty-five words in view at any time.

8. Writing long sentences and then reading them aloud tells your listeners you think they can't read. In fact, they read these long sentences quickly and lose patience and attention with your repetition.

9. Present one idea at a time.

10. If your subject is complex and requires four or five steps, do not write them all at once but write or disclose each additional step separately, leaving the others in place. This will hold interest and build to complete understanding.

HOW TO USE SLIDES AND VU-GRAPHS

Slides and Vu-Graphs are, of course, prepared in advance, and you should always rehearse when you use them to become familiar with their content and with the meeting room facilities for showing them, especially if you are going to operate the equipment yourself. If someone else will do that for you, which I think is preferable, rehearsal is essential. Devise some subtle signal between you and the operator. "Next slide, please," is the dullest sentence in the English language.

In addition, here are some special tips:

1. Place the screen in a corner of the room, not the center, for better viewing.
2. Do not darken the room completely. Keep a light on you and the room bright enough for your audience to take notes.
3. Change visuals swiftly without awkward pauses or bright flashes of light, and return to normal lighting after the presentation or during nonvisual segments of the presentation.
4. Make your introduction or explanation of the visual before presenting it, then present it and say nothing to give the audience an opportunity to absorb it before you offer any further explanation or go on to the next visual. Or to vary your presentation, show the visual and don't speak for several seconds so the audience can concentrate on it. Then say what you have to say, preferably after turning off the visual.

Remember, any visual that requires *too much* explanation is defeating its own purpose and diluting the impact of your message.

Q: What are the differences between film or videotape and other visual aids?
A: Film or videotape is more complex and more expensive—but it can be more effective.

ROLL 'EM

Film or videotapes can be great timesavers at any meeting. They speak for themselves—not only once, but as many times as you care to use them. But they can also be great time wasters if you select an inappropriate video or go to the time and expense of preparing one that just doesn't get your message across. Before you present a video or film, ask yourself these questions:

1. Is the content suitable for the occasion and the audience?
2. Is the film or tape at the right level of comprehension—neither too complex nor too elementary?
3. Should the entire film or tape be shown?
4. Would it be effective to stop the film or tape at different times to emphasize a point, to ask or answer questions, or to generate a discussion?
5. What other kind of information is necessary before, during, and after the film or tape?
6. Is there a better alternative?

If you decide to use a film, place it as near the end of the meeting as possible or your personal meeting presentation becomes anticlimactic. However, if it is the basis of the subject you want to examine and discuss, you can, of course, start with it.

AT THE CINEMA

Obviously, you need a dark room to show a film. But before you turn off the lights, explain briefly why you are showing it. An attention grabber is valuable here. For example, "Are you really safe when you travel? Here is a film that speaks louder than any words I can say on that subject." Then, lights off and begin.

Don't talk during the film—especially if you are not the one running or presenting it. When comment is required, stop the film. Sum up the key points at the conclusion of the film with the lights on and the projector off. Anything longer than thirty minutes is too long—unless you charge admission.

And don't show a film at the end of a long workday—unless it's X-rated.

> Q: How do you handle technical information at a meeting?
> A: Distribute handouts at the end of the meeting.

A DOGGIE BAG, PLEASE

If your material is highly technical, do not count on any visual or, for that matter, any spoken comment to stay in the mind of your listener or viewer. Our attention span is limited, time is required for the "decoding" of words and thoughts, and a plethora of information cannot be absorbed without a loss of facts or factors that may be crucial. Merely think of someone giving you a phone number quickly on the phone, over the radio, or on TV. If you don't write it down, you're in trouble. And don't fool yourself that technical familiarity will solve the problem, because if your listeners or viewers are that familiar with your material and know exactly what you are saying and where you're heading in advance, you shouldn't be having the meeting. So please, in these semitechnical or highly technical situations, prepare a handout and distribute it at the *completion* of the meeting or you will lose the attention of your audience as they read while you speak.

SEVEN GENERAL RULES FOR ALL VISUAL AIDS

1. A visual should emphasize an idea, clarify a concept, or illustrate a story.

2. A visual is visual. Let people look at it without disturbance.
3. A visual is meant to be seen, not read.
4. Use variety—different pictures, words, charts, bar graphs, map curves.
5. A visual can talk for you, so don't distract your listeners' attention by talking all through a visual.
6. Rehearse.
7. Present broad concepts or simplified versions of complex subjects only. If necessary, more complex or technical information should be distributed as handouts *only* at the conclusion of your presentation.

Q: What visual aid is really worth a thousand words?
A: An object.

MONEY TALKS

Bill Maier is one of the brightest young executives at Pacific Bell. He is a meeting expert. A certain prop surprised even him. In his words:

"Several years ago, when Pacific Bell was still part of AT&T and called Pacific Telephone, there was an extensive companywide effort to reduce overhead expenses. I was asked to stress with my subordinates the need for these reductions and their importance for the success of the company, and to solicit my team's support and cooperation in implementing them. Coincidentally, at that same time, I was planning to sell some of my AT&T securities. With that in mind, I carried my stock certificates to work one morning in my breast pocket to be sold after work that day.

"That same morning, I held a meeting with my subordinates to discuss the needed budget cuts. I began the meeting by urging the direct participation by all employees in these cuts. As the meeting progressed, I paced around the room making gestures to emphasize the points I was making. As a result of my pacing and gesturing I shook my stock certificates loose and they scattered all over the conference table. A hush fell over the group as they looked at the certificates and realized they were AT&T stocks. 'I'm selling them,' I said without thinking. 'Well,' said one of my subordinates, 'I guess he's really serious about those budget cuts.'

"It was an accident, but my point struck home. And that's when I realized that props can often speak louder than words."

PROPS ARE TOPS—EVEN OF MISSILES

Of course, the planned use of props is better. At a union meeting a man, without a word, held up a small piece of rubber-covered cable about five inches long and one-half inch in diameter. He paused, then after a moment said, "This is the future. This is a fiber-optic cable. Thousands of voices travel through each of the many thinner-than-a-single-hair filaments contained in this tiny piece of cable. This is the world's newest and best communications system." The room, which had not been quiet, became quiet. He had captured everyone's interest and attention.

Objects focus attention and make a point within seconds. This has been proven over and over again by the TV news. When an object has been held up, the cameras will invariably zoom in to a close shot of it. However, sometimes we must be careful with props, as evidenced by chief speech writer Donald Larson's amusing anecdote of President Dwight Eisenhower's use of a "prop":

"I was eagerly looking for something to brighten up a speech by the president and give it visual interest for the audience. By good fortune, one of the scientific breakthroughs in the space program had just taken place. Our scientists had solved the problem of achieving reentry of the nose cone of a missile into the atmosphere without its being burned up by friction with the air. I had read in the paper that the nose cone that had been successfully brought back was a sort of a prototype and not a full-size missile. In those innocent days, when most of us were not yet the experts on space vehicles that television would make us, I did not have the slightest notion of what this nose cone would look like. Undeterred by any such lack of knowledge, I decided that the highlight of the president's television speech should be his displaying the very nose cone that had been retrieved after a journey into space. I put through a call to the Pentagon, asking that the nose cone be sent over to the Oval Office. Such is the magic of a White House call, and such is the fine sense of discipline in the Pentagon, that no question was raised. I then asked one of my assistants to write a draft of an appropriate passage about the nose cone to be put in the speech.

"Sometime later I was on my way from the East Wing to the Oval Office to a meeting with the president. As I approached, I discovered that the place was in an uproar. A huge object was being maneuvered by a crew into the president's office—the nose cone, which they finally managed to wrestle into place beside the president's desk. The president said, 'Let's go over the paragraph about this thing.' No chance to change it now. Dramatically, Eisenhower read aloud the first sentence of the paragraph: 'The object *here in my hand* is a nose cone that has been to outer space and back.' "

A LITTLE BULL GOES A LONG WAY

Bill Williams of The Executive Committee (TEC) told me that his chairman in Albuquerque, New Mexico, had found a prop that provided the solution to what makes most meetings too long: digressions. He brought a tiny lead bull and during every meeting he put it in the middle of the meeting table. When somebody got long-winded, he picked up the bull and placed it directly in front of that person. It works.

A similar technique is used by a major U.S. toy manufacturing corporation. Think how many times you have said something in a meeting and somebody else said, "Yes," and then repeats exactly what you have said as if he had just thought of it. Most of the meetings I go to are full of repetition. The toy manufacturer solved that problem. They have a broken phonograph record. It has its own stand and is moved easily and quickly in front of repetitious "broken record" speakers.

Q: When should you take a risk in a meeting?
A: When it can mean a giant step forward.

BORED ROOM OR BOARDROOM

The scene is a boardroom. The surroundings are elegant. The table is enormous. The chairs are rich leather. The participants are dressed to the nines. There is a feeling of old money and elegance. The president of the company at the head of the table stands and leans forward. There is an expectant feeling in the room. The president spits on the shining mahogany conference table. No one can believe it. The president takes a handkerchief out of his pocket and wipes up the spit. "Disgusting act, wasn't it?" he says. "But you will remember it."

How right he was. Even I remember it, and I saw it years and years ago. I remember the movie the scene was in. I remember Sydney Greenstreet, the gentleman in question, and I remember the point the scene made. Greenstreet was the president of a company who wanted his advertising agency to produce more imaginative and visual ideas to sell his products, and he didn't want to waste time in long discussion.

An unusual action is memorable. It gets attention and makes a point that will stay in the mind of the listener or viewer. Don't be afraid to take a calculated risk in a meeting in order to fulfill your objective in the shortest possible time. And avoid a bored room.

A RISK MAY MEAN THE DIFFERENCE BE-TWEEN THE JACKPOT AND THE CHAMBER POT

None of us likes to look foolish in front of our peers, or our employees, or our bosses, or anybody. So, often we "settle." When a man or woman reads a speech in a meeting, he or she is settling. I'm safe, they think. What can happen? I may not look great, but I won't look bad, either. It's true they are settling—settling for mediocrity. The truly successful all take risks at least once in a while.

Picture another boardroom. Again, the surroundings are elegant. There is a large table in the center of the room and pictures of the Old West on the walls. Nine people sit around the table. The meeting is in progress. One of the gentlemen present indicates he wants to be heard. The chair acknowledges him. The gentleman rises and moves back from the table. He takes three yellow tennis balls out of his pocket and sets them down carefully so everyone can see each ball and what is painted on it in black letters. The first says "Revenue," the second "Price," and the third "Service." He picks them up and starts to juggle them. Everyone is fascinated. He speaks. "These are our issues and our problems. Which are we going to drop?" He juggles a moment longer and puts the balls down carefully as he says, "We don't have to drop any." And then he briefly presents his plan.

An excellent attention grabber, but risky. Do people accept a juggling act at a formal meeting? This man had a reputation in the company of being low profile, dignified, conservative, and dull. He recognized that this was limiting his future in the company. He must change his image and at the same time establish his real value to the company. His plan was excellent. Here was opportunity. He took the risk, and his plan was adopted. Taking a risk had created new respect and recognition for him and shortened what might have been a much longer meeting. P.S.: He practiced for days to make sure he wouldn't drop the ball.

I'LL JUMP FIRST

William Arnold III is the executive vice president of the Stanford University Hospital, one of the most highly acclaimed hospitals in the country. He is certainly part of the reason for the hospital's successful operation. Taking a calculated risk is part of his method. Let him tell you about it:

"About a month ago, I was meeting with our fourteen-member executive committee. The purpose of the meeting was to ask each committee member to reduce expenses or increase revenues by $100,000.

"During the budget meeting one executive committee member challenged me, stating that the $100,000 target was unrealistic. He began questioning the budget process and commented that this type of expense reduction and/or revenue generation was not feasible. I held my breath, then asked him whether or not I could personally add his target to my target, and if so, I would achieve his goal for him. I then asked all other members of the executive committee whether or not they wanted me to achieve their targets for them as well.

"I was taking a risk, but my response clearly set an example for the other committee members and they agreed to take on the new responsibility themselves and do their best. I got the results I wanted and increased my stature in the company."

There are important lessons to be learned from this story: Taking risks creates an opportunity for leadership, and good leadership can resolve debate, shorten the meeting, and help avoid other meetings.

DON'T BREAK THE CAMEL'S BACK

Can a conservative banker be a risk taker? Ask Tony La Scala:

"Years ago when I was a regional vice president for the Tappan Company, five other major appliance companies and Tappan were asked to make a sales presentation of our lines of cooking equipment for a major U.S. builder and his staff. I elected to make the presentation for our company. The competition was fierce because all of us knew the potential reward for the best presentation was going to be an order for over five thousand pieces of equipment, and the prestige of being selected by this influential builder was something every company wanted.

"The presentations at the meeting were all to be made on one day with each company allowed forty-five minutes maximum time to present their products. We drew numbers to see whose presentation would be first, and I drew number six which meant I would be last. At first I was thrilled at being last because I knew the last presentation would be the one that would stick in the buyer's mind. However, as the day progressed and the audience grew more weary from listening to speaker after speaker demonstrate how his product was better than the previous speaker's line, I became less excited about being last.

"When the moment of truth arrived, my turn to make the presentation, the stage curtains opened, I took one look at the audience and knew they didn't want to hear another product pitch. What do you do? I paused a few seconds and said, 'You guys don't really want to hear another product pitch, so here's mine: Everything you heard from the previous five gentlemen about the features and capabilities of their products you will find on our Tappan products— only we do it better! Now let's go have a drink.'

"I was as surprised as anyone when the very next day we were awarded the order."

Anthony La Scala is not president of the retail banking division of the Great Western Financial Corporation because he fell off a turnip truck. And I don't think he was that surprised about the results he got. He made the most of a fading situation. He sold himself, and that helped sell his product. He read his audience, took a calculated risk, and won.

BLOOD WILL TELL

I refer you to Mr. Arthur Gilbert, the distinguished collector of ancient treasures and one of the most important real estate developers in America.

"The following circumstances occurred," he told me, "when a bank wished to occupy premises on a piece of property we owned. We had a letter of intent, and based upon that, we were proceeding with the building. But the city in which the building was to be built had, in the meantime, permitted the height limit to be increased considerably. That, of course, required renewed negotiations and arrangements with the bank, and since this was the first of a number of planned regional banks to be constructed, there was no one with experience in this field in the bank. Consequently, after six months during which I attended at least two meetings a week, and at which there were always different people who wanted something additional, I finally became exasperated.

"Then on a morning that I went to my doctor for a check-up, as he was drawing some blood, I asked him to give me a very small vial with some of my blood in it. I went from there directly to yet another meeting with the bank, and once it got started and the usual negotiations commenced, I threw the vial with my blood in it on the table and said, 'Gentlemen, here's the last of it.' Recognizing the inherent finality of this humorous ploy, they concluded the lease then and there."

Thank you, Mr. Gilbert, risk king.

SIX

The Time Machine

> **Q:** How can you make a dull meeting less dull?
> **A:** Shorten it.

STANDING ROOM ONLY

One of the great merchant adventurers, or "China traders," as they were called, was William Jardine. The firm that carries his name was founded before Hong Kong and flourishes to this day. William Jardine was always conscious of time in the managing of his business. Once, at the Petition Gate in Canton, as he was conducting a transaction, he was clubbed hard on the head from behind. Jardine did not so much as turn around but finished his negotiation without losing a minute of his precious time. Thereafter he was known among the Chinese as "Iron-headed old rat," a name he perhaps rather enjoyed.

Jardine obviously knew how to handle interruptions, a great time waster at meetings. He ignored them. He used another trick to keep his meetings short. Only one chair was allowed in his Canton office. Business meetings were conducted standing—most courteously, but in minimum time.

Some 160 years later the world has changed. The clipper ships of Mr. Jardine's day no longer sail the China Seas. The days of empire are a dream of long ago. Unfortunately, meetings are not. Some seem to take 160 years. One man said to me, "The meetings I put on are so dull even I don't want to go." How do you undull a meeting? Keep it short.

Q: How can you keep a meeting from running overtime?
A: Set a time limit in advance and stick to it.

THE HANDS-ON CLOCK

A man I know had an old-fashioned alarm clock. He brought it to all his meetings and told everyone right at the beginning, "This meeting will be forty-five minutes long. When that alarm goes, I go. And when I go, you go. The meeting is over." Not only did the meeting members not resent it, they liked it and liked him for organizing everybody's time. Those meetings always ended on time.

DON'T KNOCK CONGRESS

Nate Kates, a meeting man who owns theaters and varied properties, recalls with pleasure a meeting that, he said with a grin, almost destroyed a pet belief of his. He said he had always believed business was more practical than politicians and the Congress. But he was forced to reconsider because of a government technique that worked. In Nate's words:

"We always put a time limit on our meetings and try to stick to it. But one day the meeting members were unusually verbose and it got to a couple of minutes to five. Now, five was our absolute deadline. The chairman said, 'Gentlemen, we have one more subject and vote and it's important, but we have to stop at five o'clock. What shall we do?' A loud voice from the back spoke, sarcastically but with humor, 'Let's do what Congress does—stop the clock!' "

They did, Nate told me, and the meeting ended a few minutes after five. A little humor goes a long way in a meeting. It can bring you back to reality and add energy and vitality when needed.

What if the airlines had no departure or arrival times on their schedules? There would be chaos. The same is true of meetings, and scheduling should be done as far in advance as possible and participants notified so they can plan accordingly. Always state specifically the time the meeting will begin and the time it will end. If a meeting runs over, it is usually the fault of the leader. In some cases it is unavoidable, but it is surprising what can be accomplished if there is no other choice. When your income tax final deadline is hours away—do you finish your return on time?

Q: Is there a way to minimize the amount of time each participant must spend in a meeting?

A: Stagger meeting attendance.

THE STAGGERED SOLUTION

A committee was planning a huge block party to raise money for abused children. The planning for this event took an entire year. The entertainment, the donations, the silent auction, the police permits, all required committee meetings, subcommittee meetings, and sub-subcommittee meetings. Once every two weeks, the two co-chairmen of the benefit met with their six subchairmen. To minimize the amount of time the subchairmen had to spend at the meeting, each was requested to appear at half-hour intervals: the flower chairman at 10:35, the entertainment chairman at 11:05, the clean-up chairman at 11:35, and so on, to present the current status of their individual committees. The subchairmen were invited to stay for the entire three-hour meeting *if they so desired*, but this was not mandatory. As long as they appeared at their designated time to give their updates, they were free to leave when they wished. (They never stayed.)

By staggering these reports and not requiring all six subchairmen to sit through a three-hour meeting every two weeks, the co-chairmen kept energy, enthusiasm, and commitment high, saved everybody's time, and gained reputations for efficient and productive meetings.

If you can stagger attendance at any meeting, much time is saved, both in the meeting, because each member knows the length of time allotted to conclude his business, and out of the meeting, by releasing individuals to return to work as soon as feasible.

> **Q:** How do you get participants to show up on time?
> **A:** Set an offbeat meeting time.

ODD OR EVEN

It may sound peculiar, but time management experts say we're more apt to be on time if we schedule our meetings for, say, 2:10 rather than 2:00 P.M., because 2:10 is more memorable. The more specific the time, the more likely people are to arrive promptly. When meetings are scheduled at rounded-off hours, people tend to allow an extra ten minutes before they think of themselves as being late.

> **Q:** How do you deal with latecomers?
> **A:** Wait for the decision makers; for others, it's the leader's judgment call.

EMPTY SADDLES

One of the senior executives and part owner of an international advertising agency told me that when he was a young account executive he had devised a formula that works for him to this day. When the moment to begin a meeting arrives and all are not present, do the following:

For the most important missing participant—wait. For a fairly necessary participant—wait a specific and stated length of time. For a shlump—start.

Some meeting leaders take it a step further and play hardball with latecomers. One of them suggests "at the appointed hour take all the chairs of those who have not arrived and set them outside the meeting room." Another says, "Lock the door!"

There is no single or simple answer, but there are guidelines, to be adapted to your own style and threshold of risk. You must consider the circumstances and the individual concerned. A board member of the American Psychologists Association stated, "Nothing is gained but bad feelings on all sides if a latecomer is bawled out or addressed sarcastically. It is much better merely to say—and mean it—'We're glad you're here,' and if possible, fill him in briefly on what has transpired, or merely continue the meeting. The latecomer will appreciate the courtesy and do his best to be on time for the next meeting." A city councilman, who admits he himself is often late to meetings and is embarrassed about it, suggests that the "action" is up to the latecomer. He should apologize and find his appointed seat, or one offered, as quickly and quietly as possible.

116

> **Q:** Whose job is it to keep the meeting short?
> **A:** If the leader points the way, participants will follow.

IT'S AMAZING WHAT YOUR INDEX FINGER CAN DO

Ed Kuchell, one of the top franchise experts in the country, tells this story:

"A meeting was scheduled with two attorneys, two accountants, and a merger and acquisitions consultant, as well as myself, to discuss an offer received by a large company to acquire a smaller franchising company. We had a very limited amount of time—one and a half hours to reach some sort of consensus. I was afraid that wouldn't be enough time, because in my experience attorneys, accountants, and consultants feel they have to justify the fees they're charging. And that usually means a lot of time-wasting digressions.

"So, at the start of the meeting, I explained our objective and the concern I had regarding the time. To keep the meeting on track, I requested that every time someone said anything that was not directly to the point, anyone should feel free to raise his hand with his index finger pointing upward. That would indicate that we'd better get back to the point and watch the clock.

"For the first five or ten minutes of the meeting, everyone was careful and somewhat measured with their words. But soon, when the first difference of opinion occurred, the reserved, controlled behavior faded and the digressions began. Someone raised his hand, index finger pointed upward, and an immediate silence took place. There was a certain defensiveness and an attempt to explain, whereupon another hand went up.

"From that point on, all the digressions that usually make a thirty-minute meeting take four hours disappeared. We accomplished our task in the prescribed one and a half hours. And as an added bonus, each one of us left that meeting with a greater respect for each other and for ourselves."

By giving joint responsibility to the meeting members, everyone shared control and Ed got the result he wanted with a shorter meeting.

Q: How do you keep a meeting on track?
A: Discuss only one issue at a time.

RIDE THE PARLOR CAR TOGETHER

A group of people were meeting to plan their upcoming fund-raiser. The topic for discussion was whether or not to serve refreshments. Here's how it went:

"I vote for ice cream."

"We'd need several sauces, maybe a make-your-own sundae table. I could provide the nuts."

"I'm allergic to chocolate. We need at least two other flavors."

"I have a little ice-cream maker. How much would it cost to make homemade ice cream for a hundred people? How about pistachio?"

"Are we sure we want ice cream in December? What about a special cake made in the shape of an endangered species?"

"Everyone's on a diet—let's serve coffee and celery."

Needless to say, nothing was accomplished at that meeting.

The most important consideration in keeping a large meeting on track is to discuss only *one* question at a time. In the above exchange, the participants have still to decide whether or not to serve refreshments at all. What kind, what cost, what flavor, who brings the nuts, are irrelevant at this point because the first question has not yet been decided. This is where knowledge of parliamentary procedures, even in a very simplified form, is invaluable.

Robert's Rules of Order is the standard guideline to parliamentary procedures. Here are four of them that can keep any large meeting, especially those in which questions are going to be debated by a considerable number of attendees, as concise and to the point as possible.

Heads and Tails

1. Present both sides of the question. Should the church sell part of its parking lot? Should the PTA allocate funds to project A or project B? Should the Ballet Guild increase its membership or increase its yearly dues? Each member who speaks in favor of selling the parking lot should be followed by a speaker who is against selling it. Each comment in favor of funding project A should be followed by someone preferring project B.

The Stopwatch

2. Limit the length of time that a speaker may have the floor—ten minutes, five minutes, two minutes—whatever length of time seems appropriate to the length of the meeting and the number of attendees.

Three's a Crowd

3. Limit the number of times a speaker may speak on *any given question* to twice. This does not mean twice in the meeting, it means twice on any individual question.

Even a Duel Needs Seconds

4. Once a question has been discussed, a motion is made to take further action. Verify that there is sufficient support for a motion. If only one member out of a thousand wants to paint the clubhouse blue, the management committee should not spend hours obtaining estimates. If a motion is not seconded—if no one else is in favor of the proposed action—it is not discussed further. If the motion is seconded, it is put to a vote. Seconds to a motion, or letters or petitions with a specified number of signatories, indicate whether there is sufficient backing for any question to be discussed in a meeting. Remember, seconds save seconds—and hours.

Q: When should you interrupt?
A: When you want to take the floor and gain control.

EXCUSE ME, BUT . . .

Interrupting is a gentle art unto itself. We do it and have it done to us every day of our lives and take it as a matter of course. It isn't. It is a technique and is used consciously or unconsciously to achieve a purpose. Interrupting is a meeting tool. It is a method of taking the floor and gaining control. Not allowing interruptions holds the floor and control.

GRABBING THE BALL

What are some of the methods of interrupting? One is to raise your hand and say, "Just a second, may I . . ." and continue speaking. Another way to interrupt is to stand. The person speaking will usually pause, and calling that person by name, you can say, "John, there's something else," and continue speaking. You can also just speak, raising the level of your voice above the person speaking. Be sure, however, that when you ask permission to interrupt you don't wait for permission to be granted but continue directly to your message.

One of the most difficult things to do in a brisk meeting is to hold back and allow others to finish presenting what you consider to be incorrect assumptions and actions when you *know* you have the right and perfect answer to the problem. I have had the urge to jump in and interrupt a thousand times and have done so in many cases. Or I have waited for the briefest pause and then moved in. This is not the best of business manners. Also, it can be embarrassing if, as has happened to me, your perfect point is not perfect and was thought of and discarded long ago. Think twice before making yourself vulnerable by interrupting the speaker.

Interruptions can lead to digressions, which prolong the length of a meeting. But a polite interruption that *cuts off* a digression is an excellent way to save time.

Q: How do you prevent yourself from being interrupted?

A: *Insist* on finishing your point.

THE MEEK DO NOT INHERIT THE EARTH

It is crucial in a meeting to be able to prevent someone from interrupting you. When, as a participant, you are making your point at a meeting and someone interrupts you, you lose control and the opportunity to present your point. If you are sure of what you are saying and have your concise effective statement under way, do not accept interruptions. When someone says, "May I . . . " and starts to talk, just say, "Please, hold your thought," and continue. Or say, "Just a sec," and continue; or say, "Please, just let me finish. . . ." and continue. In an adversary situation, if someone interrupts, speak louder. If he speaks louder, you speak louder still. And if he speaks louder again, just stop and say nothing. He will look foolish and know it and you will win. Another effective method when you are interrupted is just to hold up your hand, palm out, and continue speaking.

No matter how politely you interrupt someone, *don't let anyone interrupt you*—no matter how politely. It is absolutely essential for meeting participants to be able to finish statements. Especially if the statements are concise, carefully thought out, and well prepared. These statements can, and will, be the key to your meeting success. Keep in mind your message can be bright, brief, and beautiful but totally useless if you don't get it across.

> **Q:** How do you handle destructive criticism?
> **A:** Make the critic prove his point.

UNCOMMON SENSE

Some people interrupt, ask adversary questions, and just plain disrupt meetings in order to show how much they know or to gain authority. Larry Kitchen, the recently retired chairman of Lockheed, is an expert in knowing what to do in these situations. Here's a technique that works wonders for him:

"When I was a young department manager, I saw a sign in a small curio shop that helped me correct an irritating problem that had been disrupting my weekly staff meetings.

"Several of the staff members had developed the time-consuming habit of cross-examining their colleagues after each presentation, regardless of how well the subject was presented and supported. Although these inquiries were always made under the guise of obtaining clarification or additional information, they were often hostile and counterproductive.

"After enduring this situation for a few weeks, I remembered that sign in the curio shop, which read 'You break it, you buy it.' I decided to apply this rule at my next staff meeting. Following a particularly derisive exchange, I addressed the harshest critic, saying, 'Steve, you seem to have serious concerns about this issue. At our next meeting, I'd like you to present a thorough analysis of this proposal—along with three or four workable alternatives.' It took exactly two applications of this technique to cure the inquisitors of their negative conduct. The net result was a significant saving of conference time and a welcome increase in productivity."

> **Q:** How do you stop people from making meet-
> ings interminable by gnawing at every detail?
> **A:** Create a subcommittee and invite the gnawers
> to gnaw at *their* meeting.

FOR GNAWERS ONLY

Ken Todd ran a first-rate public relations operation
for AT&T on the West Coast. At the same time he was
involved in charities all over the country. I felt sorry
for him because of the continual meetings he was
subjected to. But I really didn't have to feel sorry, as
you will see by the way Ken handles "gnawers":

"Many of the charitable boards I sit on meet at
night because that's the only time members are
available. And many a night I've had to sit on a hard
oak chair (it's usually donated furniture) for five
hours listening to very good people (the salt of the
earth, in fact) gnawing over the small details of the
treasurer's report for the Urban League. But since it
was my good fortune to be chairman of this board
(fortunate in that I had control, unfortunate in that I
couldn't just get up and leave), I could make changes.

"I instituted a finance committee, made up of
board people with high qualifications in accounting
and budget work. Then I pointed out to the board

that the treasurer's report would be analyzed by this committee, recommended for passage by this talented group only when they were satisfied, and passed by the full board with minimum discussion.

"At the next meeting, when a little gnawing started, I ruled that the matter needed no discussion and that anyone interested could attend the finance committee meeting. This move not only shortened the meeting, it also gave me a system for setting up further committees on other contentious matters the board had to deal with. And that made our board meetings so brisk and efficient that attendance rose nicely.

"And none of the gnawers ever attended the finance committee meetings!"

Ken didn't just head off time-wasting questions from people unfamiliar with special areas under discussion. Or even merely stop people who gnaw at every detail and make meetings interminable. Far more important, he put qualified people in the right place to do the right job and get the fastest results. And above all, he got an extra hour of sleep.

Q: If your meeting members are not experts on a subject under consideration, how can you provide answers and save time?

A: Get an expert to come to the meeting.

THE HORSE'S MOUTH

A sixty-five-year-old church in Los Angeles needed a new roof. The board of directors obtained estimates and called a meeting of the entire church membership to recommend acceptance of one of the bids. Anticipating the many legitimate questions that could be raised at this meeting, they requested the owner of the recommended company to be present. For half an hour he explained procedures, described what the proposed process would entail, discussed how much it would cost and why, and expertly answered every question posed by members. He was then thanked, excused, and a vote was taken to go ahead with the work.

A computer software company was preparing their first user's manual. No expense was being spared in the writing and design. The president of the company requested the head of the publications division to meet with him to describe what the book was going to look like. She met with him—but she didn't describe the manual. She brought along the graphic artist she had hired, who had made a mock-up of the book and could answer questions, incorporate changes, and explain the reasoning behind the design.

In both cases the meeting leaders, realizing that much time would be wasted trying to respond to questions they were not qualified to answer, went to the horse's mouth, saving themselves research and shortening the length of the actual meeting. If you have an expert on a subject, use him. If you don't, find one. And remember, unanswered or deferred questions mean more meetings.

Q: How can you shorten the decision-making process?
A: Vote.

HANDS UP

The real test of the success of any meeting is that the necessary decisions are "signed, sealed, and delivered." And often the best way to accomplish that is to put it to a vote.

ANALYSIS = PARALYSIS

Phil Quigley, president of Pacific Bell and former head of the very successful mobile access operation of Pacific Telesis in California—car phones to us nontechnical people—says:

> More old analysis
> Leads to paralysis.

What he means is, make the decision even if you don't have every fact known to exist. Face it, people do not like to make decisions. We like to sit on the fence. We think "no decision" can keep us out of trouble. Just one word is the perfect answer to that time waster: vote. Whenever the discussion is endless at a meeting, just whisper to the meeting leader, "Vote." If he's a good leader, he'll love you for it.

If you cannot for whatever reason take a vote, suggest a straw vote. A straw vote is a "sample" vote that gives an indication but does not commit to the subject in question. If the vote is close, more discussion is in order, but if not, you are in a much stronger position to call for the real vote.

Q: What prolongs meetings by resisting logic?
A: Emotion.

DEALING WITH EMOTION

A small business group held a meeting to determine whether to move and rent space on the thirty-fourth floor of a new thirty-five-story building in New York City. At the time they had offices on the ground floor of an old building in a recently depressed neighborhood where they had been for over ten years. The move required unanimous approval of the seven people present. There were many good reasons to make the change. However, one man resisted, taking the position, "Why change a winning game? We're doing fine where we are. Why spend more money?"

It was pointed out that the expenditure would be a good investment in the future. The man wouldn't accept that. His associates presented sound and solid facts and figures and clear logic as to why his position was unreasonable. The more the merits of the deal were presented—the gain in value, the better neighborhood—the more he seemed to resist.

Unknown to the rest of the participants, the reasons he resisted were emotional. As a child he had been in a hotel fire. Smoke and flames had terrified him, and it seemed forever until he was taken down from the twentieth floor in an elevator. The elevator got stuck between floors, and the nightmare seemed never to end. From that point on he was always nervous in elevators and counted the seconds between floors.

He walked out of the meeting without telling his associates why he was so opposed to the move. There were ill feelings and nothing was accomplished. Perhaps there was no solution right then, but a lot of time and effort might have been saved if it had been recognized that the problem was emotional and could not be handled with logic.

LOGIC LOSES IN EMOTIONAL SITUATIONS

Inside or outside any meeting, the best way to get good results is to be objective and focus your thinking toward achieving your goal. Emotions are the dark or bright clouds that obscure your thinking process. Recognize that logic loses to emotion. No matter how long the meeting, you cannot convince a person with logic if his mind is blocked by emotion. And further recognize that your logic may not be logical at all to your emotional listener, because the problem you feel is causing his reaction and which you are addressing may not be *the* problem at all— and usually isn't. As in the case of the man who did not want to work in a high-rise building, all the logical reasons for moving did not address the real reasons for his resistance.

> **Q:** How do you handle a person in an emotional state?
> **A:** Make him aware of his feelings, get him to talk, and don't criticize him.

TALK-TALK-TALK

There are times when a long meeting is actually short and saves time. It depends on results. A short meeting with no result is a total waste of time. And without exception, meetings that do not accomplish anything lead to more meetings. To focus and fulfill a meeting objective generally involves logic and clear thinking on behalf of all concerned. People in an emotional state do not think clearly and are seldom logical.

The best way to handle such people is to try to make them aware of their emotions. Ask them why they feel the way they do. Get them to talk, to express their feelings. It will relieve the pressure on everybody. But don't criticize them for being emotional. Making them aware of their emotions is as far as you should go. If that technique had been applied to the gentleman who was afraid of elevators, he might have changed his mind about moving to the new building. Certainly a lot of time would have been saved. You should try to apply that same technique to your own emotional reactions. Try to recognize them for what they are and keep them under control.

Meetings are high-pressure situations, and emotions can sometimes run high. But expressing strong negative emotions is almost counterproductive—not to mention time-consuming. Negative emotions can be contagious. Everybody begins to dig in his heels, and the meeting comes to a complete standstill. If that happens, you'll actually save time by taking a break to let things cool down or finding a pretext to reschedule the meeting.

Q: What is the biggest meeting time waster of all?
A: Fighting losing battles.

TWELVE O'CLOCK LOW

Twentieth Century–Fox was getting ready to start a motion picture called *Twelve O'Clock High*. It was a big one, and Gregory Peck had been signed to play the lead. At the time, I represented Charles Bickford, a fine and important character actor. The second leading role in the film was open, and I got them to offer it to Bickford. They met his salary demand, which was a lot of money, and offered co-star billing with Peck, but Bickford's name would be 75 percent of the size of Peck's name on the screen and in paid advertising.

Bickford read the script, liked it, and called me.

"I'll do it," he said, "if they give me the same-size billing as Peck—not 75 percent but 100 percent."

I called the studio and they said no. I told Bickford. He said, "Sorry, kid. I want my name in the same-size letters as Peck."

The studio wouldn't budge. They couldn't; they said they were contractually obligated to Peck on the billing. I tried Bickford again, but he insisted on the 100 percent billing. After a couple of weeks the studio said to me, "Look, tell Bickford to make up his mind, yes or no. We'll give you forty-eight hours, then if we don't hear anything, we'll get someone else." I called Bickford and we had a lunch meeting. I asked him to reconsider. He mustn't lose the part over a 25 percent difference in the size of his name on the screen. "Kid," he said, "no 75 percent. If they'll give me 100 percent, I'll do it."

I was desperate because I knew it was now or never. "Mr. Bickford," I said, "you've got to accept the billing and do the part. You can't win this billing battle. They're contractually obligated to Peck. Don't fight a losing battle when you can still win the war." I paused, then said, "If you play that part, you'll win the Academy Award." And I meant it.

Bickford looked at me quizzically and said, "No. I'll only do it on my terms." He refused to accept the inevitable. The studio stood firm. Dean Jagger played the part and won the Academy Award. Bickford fired me, and I didn't blame him. As far as he was concerned, I hadn't been able to get him what he wanted.

You must read your "audience" at any meeting. You must try to judge just how far you can go in order to achieve your main objective. Bickford didn't do that. He fought and continued to fight a losing battle and lost not only that battle and the Academy Award, but the future opportunity that award offered, to get any billing he wanted opposite any star. Measure your chances of success in every situation. If it looks impossible, there is always another day— and fortunately, or unfortunately, another meeting.

Incidentally, Bickford never won an Academy Award, nor, in spite of many fine performances, was he even nominated.

> **Q:** When do you end a meeting?
> **A:** When the objective has been accomplished, conclude.

WHEN IT'S OVER, IT'S OVER

Arthur and Richard Pine, two fine literary agents, never seemed to have enough time because of wasted time spent in many business meetings. But they have considerably more time now, through the use of the technique illustrated in this story from Arthur Pine:

"A couple of years ago Richard and I attended the final meeting to consummate a deal with Orion Pictures for one of the novels we were representing or else to call off further negotiations. In attendance at this meeting were six or seven top executives of Orion and Chairman of the Board Arthur Krim. I would estimate that meeting, which involved several hundreds of thousands of dollars, did not take more than fifteen minutes, because Mr. Krim, who incidentally has been adviser to several presidents of the United States, was prepared to ask Richard and myself the pertinent questions about the book involved and why Richard and I (agents for the author) felt it was worth the money we were asking. Once we gave Mr. Krim our reasons, he asked his other executives if they had any further questions, and when they replied, 'No,' he said to Richard and me, 'Gentlemen, you have a deal. Thank you for attending this meeting.' He then shook our hands and left the meeting room immediately while the other Orion executives stayed on to chat with us.

"Richard and I were very impressed and learned the lesson that once the objective of a meeting has been accomplished, bring it to a polite but firm conclusion and do not get into any additional business discussions. Knowing when to stop is sometimes more important than knowing when to start. If you want to hang around and socialize to cement relationships, by all means do so. But you should recognize that such socializing serves a different purpose."

SEVEN

Video Teleconferencing

> **Q:** Why should you know the pros and cons of video teleconferencing?
>
> **A:** Because it's here to stay, and few people know how to make the best use of it.

LIGHTS, CAMERA, ACTION!

A video teleconference is a meeting where you can't shake hands—at least not physically.

The biggest pro of video teleconferencing is the time it saves. The very nature of purchasing a time slot and a specific number of minutes on the air forces careful thought on how to get the most for your buck. I have yet to attend a teleconference meeting where anyone was late or where the meeting ran over the allotted time. The following pros and cons speak for themselves:

Pros

• Conserves time
• Reduces travel and travel expenses
• Speeds up decision making
• Gives expanded access to key people and data around the world

Cons

• No personal contact
• Can create false impressions
• Requires special skills to perform on camera
• Technical difficulties

Video teleconferencing may be on the cutting edge of modern-day communications, but the steps you should take to prepare for an effective video presentation are exactly the same as the preparatory steps for a good old-fashioned meeting.

1. Set objectives and prepare written agenda.
2. Select and confirm all attendees.

3. Schedule teleconferencing rooms and equipment for the time required.
4. Distribute agendas and teleconference rules to all participants.
5. Confirm agenda well in advance.
6. Prepare necessary visual aids.
7. Confirm where and how they will be used.

Q: What is the major difference between teleconferencing and any other type of meeting?

A: You are on camera.

SO YOU WANNA BE IN PICTURES!

Two senior executives from a Detroit manufacturing company interviewed a gentleman for a high-level job with their company. Because the person being interviewed couldn't come to Detroit at that time, they decided to hold the interview meeting through a video teleconference. It was the first time the person had been interviewed in front of a video camera. Usually he was effective in meetings, but he was not comfortable in front of a camera and it showed. He looked down when he spoke, which made him appear devious, and his sentences were slow and rambling. Nervousness made him perspire, adding to the unfortunate impression. Unfair or not, he didn't get the job.

YOU'RE IT

Video teleconferencing is a growing medium where, in a sense, you become the visual aid. And just as you are not born with the ability to communicate brilliantly, so you are not born knowing how best to utilize video communicating. You must learn to make the medium work for you rather than the other way around.

First and foremost, you are going to be on television. Cameras and lights will probably intimidate you, at least at first. That is a natural reaction. You also know that at some point you are going to be shown in close-up—the "star" of the show—and the heavens will fall if you make a mistake. These "horrors" can be easily handled with the proper preparation and a few techniques that will help you present you and your message effectively.

APPEARANCE COUNTS

To present the persuasive and eloquent person we all want to be does take a bit more than just sitting on the edge of your chair and not chewing gum or smoking. Your appearance, your dress, and your manner of self-presentation are all vital factors in effective video teleconferencing.

Man or woman, as far as your personal appearance is concerned, go to the experts who know how to make you look your best on camera. That includes your hairstyle, makeup, and dress. People actually look different on camera than in person. Depending on the camera angle and lighting, you can look thinner or heavier, older or younger. Too much makeup ages you. The way you dress also changes your appearance. White is the worst color to wear; the camera must adjust to it and in so doing darkens your face. Wear off-white, gray, blue, any color but white. Also, be careful with plaids and busy patterns, which shimmer and vibrate on camera and take attention away from you and your message.

Duck into the restroom just before you go on camera to make sure you look your best. You also have to consider the lights, which can be very hot, and you should dress accordingly. And don't wear any jewelry that may reflect the lights or cause distracting noises on the microphone. Seeking expert advice on all these matters is not very expensive because you only have to do it once. Nor is it all that technical or complicated. With a little experience, you can become an expert yourself. When you know you look good it makes you feel good and you do a better job of communicating effectively off camera as well as on.

ZOMBIES LOSE

When you speak on camera you become the center of attention. The camera focuses on you and generally zooms in for a close shot. The video screen frames you in the same way a photograph or painting is framed. Without the distraction of your surroundings, the viewer's attention is concentrated solely on your face. Your movements and expressions are magnified. This can work for you or against you. A nonanimated, nonsmiling face tends to look serious, cold, and uncaring. A smile does wonders. Variety of expression is an absolute must. Sitting on the edge of your seat is especially important when you are on camera. It slants your body forward comfortably, giving you energy and conviction. Above all, be natural and speak in your normal tone of voice. Again, seek the advice of experts. Practice is also useful. You can play back a practice video of yourself and see exactly what you look and sound like to others. If you don't like it, practice until you get it right.

BIG BROTHER

In a video studio there is usually more than one camera. The question is which one is looking at you. Often the camera is voice-activated. You speak and you are on camera. When someone else speaks he is on and you are not. But be careful. When there is a pause in conversation, within ten seconds a camera will go to a two-shot or wider (two or more participants will be seen on the screen), and one of them may be you. A most important rule is, "Always assume you are on camera and act accordingly." Blowing your nose or straightening your tie when you think you are not on camera can prove to be very embarrassing.

Because TV cameras are set up differently in different rooms, you must find the person in charge and ask if you should talk into the video camera or to the video monitor, which displays the people to whom you are talking. Otherwise it is like not looking at someone when you speak to them. You will appear shifty and lose credibility.

> **Q:** When should you take notes to a teleconference meeting?
> **A:** Always.

WHO'S LOOKING?

When I do radio or TV interviews, talk shows, or teleconferences, I always take notes with me. I just lay them down on the table, and they are noticeable to no one but me. The camera usually doesn't pick up the tabletop, and the camera person will go out of his or her way, as well, to avoid your "white paper notes." In the actual interview I never speak while I am looking down at the notes. I only speak while I am looking at the other people present. No one in the audience even knows I am using notes.

Notes keep you on track and help you say exactly what you want in the shortest possible time.

TEN RULES FOR THE TELECONFERENCE LEADER

1. Start on time.
2. Repeat start and finish time.

3. Review objectives, ground rules, and who is present.
4. Encourage participation and help those who are new.
5. Use questions to stimulate discussion.
6. Use visuals as planned
7. Insure everyone gets equal time or time as set out by agenda.
8. Summarize and clarify key points.
9. Hold to the agenda to keep meeting on track.
10. At the time of the teleconference meeting, summarize important decisions, key assignments, and follow-up actions.

TEN RULES FOR TELECONFERENCE PARTICIPANTS

1. Use concise statements to make your point.
2. State your name at least the first time you speak.
3. Use other participants' names—imagine they are sitting right across from you.
4. Don't carry on side conversations without muting your microphone. (Put your hand over it, gently.)
5. Direct questions to specific individuals or locations.
6. Spell out unusual terms, names, and numbers.

147

7. Use verbal pointers: "Please remember this," "You might want to write this down," and so on.
8. Use gestures—they give energy and vitality. But be careful of quick movements; they sometimes blur.
9. Don't watch yourself on the monitor as you speak.
10. Relax and be yourself.

THE BOTTOM LINE

In an ordinary meeting we usually do not think of the time of the individuals concerned—those sitting in the meeting—as costing real dollars. Knowing you are actually paying money—real hard dollars—to use the teleconference room and equipment has a focusing effect. Keeping the value of time in mind makes you prepare more carefully. Every person present at the meeting represents time and money spent. Each tick of the clock adds to the cost. The video teleconference may involve special equipment and facilities, but video conference techniques will help you save time in any meeting situation.

EIGHT

The End of Meetings and the Aftermath

> **Q:** What is the difference between stimulating discussions and a productive meeting?
> **A:** Results.

HURRAH!

Harold Gershowitz, senior vice president and chairman of his company's legislative and regulatory policy committee, sent me this case history:

"The purpose of my committee is to review legislative and regulatory proposals as they evolve throughout the United States and to develop a corporate position with respect to these issues. We used to meet monthly and, because of the numerous alternatives and variations of these issues, a great deal of time was wasted on stimulating but inconclusive discussion.

"To solve that problem, I assigned staff to condense the issues in a discussion paper to be distributed one week prior to the LRPC meeting. The format of the meeting was changed so that only items requiring a final decision would be on the agenda. Now the meeting members are conversant with the various alternative positions when they come to the meeting, and discussion is reduced substantially. The length of the meetings is shortened considerably with a commensurate increase in the productivity of each session.

"I feel that meetings involving long, rambling discussions are seldom productive. Committee members should come to the meeting ready to vote. Formal meetings are not rap sessions. They are for decision making."

Mr. Gershowitz's meeting procedure could win an Oscar for the most consistently concise and productive meetings of the year. Let's break down the steps:

1. The meeting objective is clear.
2. Advance preparation is made on issues to be discussed by qualified staff.
3. Discussion papers of the meeting are prepared

and delivered one week in advance of the meeting
to committee members.

4. Only "final decision" items requiring a vote are
   permitted on the agenda.
5. Committee members are prepared.
6. Discussion is limited.
7. A vote is taken.

You, too, should recognize the subtle but important difference between stimulating discussions and
productive meetings. By following these same steps
before and during any meeting, you can improve productivity and cut the meeting time to less than half.

Q: If your meeting is unsuccessful, what should
you do?
A: Change your tactics.

ABOUT-FACE

Jeremy P. Tarcher, a successful independent pub-
lisher, holds regular editorial staff meetings. The simple objective of these staff meetings is to present
publishing proposals. He had three meetings in a row

in which nothing was presented. That was enough time wasted. He reevaluated and recognized his problem. So many manuscripts were being submitted from authors and smaller literary agents that no one was really out on the town looking for that one-in-a-million bestseller. Tarcher knew many powerful literary agents were going directly to the big publishers and making deals before he ever had access to the best manuscripts they represented. He rethought his goal and plan and took positive action. He held a short fourth meeting and asked each of the fifteen people present to call two literary agents starting right after the conclusion of the meeting in order to try and get their top product. This was a new procedure. The result was that at the next meeting they had a book to publish. *Women Who Love Too Much* by Robin Norwood sold a quarter of a million copies in hardcover and two million paperback copies.

Q: How can you best evaluate the success of your meeting?
A: Ask participants for their written opinions.

EVERYBODY WINS

It is vital to determine the value of any meeting. At the end of *every* meeting the objective should be restated and the results of the meeting summarized. Also restate any assignments that have been made and the follow-up actions required.

In order to evaluate further, ask each participant to give his opinion of the meeting in writing, including brief answers to the following questions, and return his comments to the meeting leader within seventy-two hours:

1. Did we achieve the meeting objective as stated in the agenda?
2. If not, why not?
3. What three positive things can we do to improve the next meeting?
4. What are three things we did that we should not do at the next meeting?
5. What are the two most important things the leader can do to improve the meeting?
6. What are the two most important things the participants can do to improve the meeting?
7. Could we have done without this meeting?
8. If so, how?

The answers to the above will give you a clear picture of the effectiveness of the meeting from the participants' point of view. It will also increase involvement and responsibility of all participants. Better and briefer meetings will result.

EPILOGUE

The Last Word

THE ULTIMATE IN HIGH-TECH DEVICES

I have always believed in science fiction. In my recent work at the Kennedy Space Center I have seen those visions come true.

The platforms that hold the various orbiters are enormous. The fuel tanks and payloads are a wonder. The hangar containing these miracles has a height, it is said, that allows clouds to form beneath the ceiling. I saw the orbiter *Discovery*. Charlie Floyd of Lockheed asked me if I would like to inspect the inside of the cabin. He had never been in the cabin himself. With the needed approval, we put on the shoes, hats, and bunny suits requisite for boarding or working on the spacecraft. We climbed the stairs to peer inside this vehicle of man's destiny. There were two men working in the tiny cabin. They helped me crawl through the narrow opening and asked if I would like to sit in the command pilot's seat.

I sat in the tiny seat. The lights in the cabin went down. The instrument panel came on. I looked out of the small window in front of me and dreamed of the courage and will that took man into space. My heart beat faster as in my mind I sensed the blackness of space our astronauts encountered when they were thrust into the void. I have doubts about many things mankind has done, but there is greatness in our daring exploration of space.

Later I talked to Bill Brett, who runs a major operation at Kennedy Space Center. I admired his leadership and the great technological work of his group. How did they do it? I wanted to know if, with the amount of detail, technical data, and planning involved, their meetings weren't endless. "Sometimes," he said. "But at Kennedy Space Center we have developed a high-tech device to focus, tighten, and shorten our meetings."

He took a silver box out of his drawer, opened it, and handed me a thin flat plywood square with two holes in it: the Kennedy Space Center Thumb Twiddler.

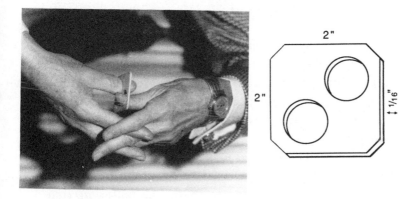

When meetings wandered, got off track, and lost sight of their objectives, Brett told me he or another participant would put his right thumb in one hole and his left thumb in the other hole from the opposite side, intertwine his fingers, and rotate the Twiddler. Those watching got the point and the meeting was soon back on track.

If you're curious to try it out, it takes only a minute or two to manufacture this ingenious high-tech object out of a piece of cardboard or even a narrow strip of plywood. It will save *many* minutes when you demonstrate its use the next time one of your meetings begins to wander. I have used the Twiddler. It works. It may not get you into space, but I guarantee it will keep your meetings on track.

IF ALL ELSE FAILS . . .

In the seventeenth century, an edict was passed by the lord protector of England, Oliver Cromwell, that in order to curtail the savage practices of some of his troops (ranging from rape to pillage and murder), a new procedure would be initiated. The offending soldier and his entire company would assemble underneath the local gallows and hold a meeting. This meeting, in main, would consist of the rolling of dice. Everyone would participate. The man who lost would be hanged. Not necessarily the instigator of the crime, but simply the man who lost. The results were fewer crimes, fewer troops—and fewer meetings.

BECOME A COMMUNICATIONS GENIUS!

Listen in as Milo Frank, renowned communications expert, shows you how to develop effective meeting strategies and communication skills to get you started on the road to success!

Whether you are a leader or a participant, using valuable time efficiently can mean a more successful and fulfilling future for you, and Milo O. Frank provides you with the important tools to do it!

HOW TO RUN
A SUCCESSFUL MEETING—IN HALF THE TIME

You've read the book, now let Milo Frank enhance what you've learned. Listen in as many times as you need as he provides the proven strategies for planning and conducting meetings for greater productivity and success to get the results you want quickly.
#5400, $9.95 (Running Time: 50 Minutes)

HOW TO GET YOUR
POINT ACROSS IN 30 SECONDS – OR LESS

In this program, Milo Frank offers techniques for communicating clearly and more effectively in a shorter span of time. From writing letters, giving speeches, asking for a promotion or closing a sale, here are invaluable methods for learning how to get exactly what you want every time you ask for it.
#5003, $9.95 (Running Time: 45 Minutes)

About the Author

Milo O. Frank is a nationally acclaimed authority on communications skills and strategies. His proven techniques have brought him success in an extraordinary career as an actors' agent, the Director of Talent and Casting for CBS Television, a writer-producer of feature films at MGM, and vice president in charge of production for Cinerama. For many years, he has taught the secrets of better communication to business people and politicians, and is a much-sought-after lecturer and seminar leader in America and throughout the Pacific Rim. His classic book, *How to Get Your Point Across in 30 Seconds—Or Less,* has been a perennial best-seller, and has been phenomenally successful as an audiocassette program as well. Mr. Frank lives with his wife in Beverly Hills, California.